Airbnb Mortgage Loan Refinancing & Cash-Out Strategies

How to Refinance Airbnb Properties and Pull Out Equity to Scale Faster

By Joseph G. Correa

Licensed Mortgage Broker, Finibi Mortgage

Copyright & Legal Notice

Published by Live Stronger Faster

The information provided in this book is for educational and informational purposes only and should not be construed as financial, legal, or tax advice. Readers are encouraged to consult with licensed professionals before making any financial or real estate decisions. The author and publisher assume no responsibility for any losses or damages incurred as a result of the use or misuse of the information contained in this publication.

First Edition, 2026

Table of Contents

Foreword

Refinancing is not simply about lowering an interest rate or adjusting loan terms. In the context of Airbnb and short-term rental investing, refinancing becomes a strategic tool for accessing trapped equity, improving cash flow, and repositioning assets for long-term growth. As your properties appreciate in value and generate consistent income, they begin to hold untapped financial potential. This potential, when properly accessed through cash-out refinancing or rate-and-term refinancing, allows you to reinvest without relying solely on new savings or external capital. In essence, your existing portfolio becomes the engine that funds your future acquisitions. This concept, often referred to as equity recycling, is one of the most powerful wealth-building strategies available in real estate today.

One of the core strategies explored in this book is the cash-out refinance. This method allows you to replace your existing mortgage with a new, larger loan based on the current value of the property, while receiving the difference in cash. For Airbnb investors, this is particularly impactful because short-term rental properties often appreciate faster due to their income-producing potential. Unlike traditional long-term rentals, Airbnb properties can command higher valuations when supported by strong revenue data. This means that as you optimize your listing, improve occupancy rates, and increase your average daily rate, you are not just boosting cash flow—you are actively increasing your property's refinance potential.

Closely tied to the cash-out refinance is the BRRRR strategy, which stands for Buy, Rehab, Rent, Refinance, Repeat. While this strategy has traditionally been associated with long-term rentals, it has evolved significantly in the short-term rental space. In the Airbnb model, the "rent" phase is replaced with a high-performing short-term rental operation, often generating significantly higher income than a standard lease. This increased income can lead to higher appraised values, especially when lenders consider DSCR or income-based valuation methods. By executing the BRRRR strategy with Airbnb properties, investors can recover a large portion—sometimes all—of their initial capital, allowing them to reinvest into additional properties without depleting their reserves.

However, refinancing Airbnb properties is not without its complexities. Lenders evaluate these properties differently, often requiring a deeper understanding of income stability, market trends, and property performance. Unlike traditional loans that rely heavily on borrower income, many Airbnb refinance options—especially DSCR loans—focus on the property's ability to generate sufficient income to cover its debt obligations. This shifts the emphasis from personal financials to property performance. As a result, investors must be prepared to present strong documentation, including rental history, occupancy data, and market analysis. Understanding how to position your property in the best possible light can make the difference between a successful refinance and a missed opportunity.

Another critical component of refinancing strategy is timing. Knowing when to refinance is just as important as knowing how. Refinancing too early may limit your ability to extract meaningful equity, while waiting too long could expose you to market risks such as rising interest rates or declining property values. Strategic investors monitor key indicators such as property appreciation, income growth, and market conditions to determine the optimal moment to refinance. In many cases, even small improvements in property performance—such as better reviews, enhanced amenities, or optimized pricing—can significantly impact valuation and loan eligibility.

Equity recycling is where the true power of refinancing becomes evident. Instead of allowing equity to remain idle within a property, investors can extract it and redeploy it into new acquisitions. This creates a compounding effect, where each property contributes to the growth of the portfolio. Over time, this strategy can transform a single property into a multi-property portfolio, all funded by the equity generated along the way. This is not just a theoretical concept—it is the blueprint used by many of the most successful real estate investors. By mastering equity recycling, you are no longer limited by your initial capital. Instead, your portfolio becomes self-sustaining and continuously expanding.

Risk management is also a crucial aspect of refinancing and cash-out strategies. While accessing equity provides tremendous opportunities, it also introduces new responsibilities. Increasing loan balances can impact cash flow, especially if not carefully structured. Investors must ensure that their properties continue to generate sufficient income to cover higher debt obligations while maintaining a margin for expenses, vacancies, and unforeseen challenges. This is where disciplined underwriting and conservative projections become essential. The goal is not just to grow quickly, but to grow sustainably.

Additionally, this book explores the differences between various refinance options, including rate-and-term refinances, cash-out refinances, and portfolio-level refinancing strategies. Each option serves a different purpose and is suited to different stages of an investor's journey. For example, a rate-and-term refinance may be ideal for improving cash flow by securing a lower interest rate, while a cash-out refinance is more focused on extracting equity for reinvestment. Understanding when and how to use each strategy allows you to tailor your approach based on your goals and market conditions.

As you progress through this book, you will begin to see refinancing not as a one-time event, but as an ongoing strategy integrated into your overall investment plan. The most successful Airbnb investors treat refinancing as a routine part of their portfolio management, continuously optimizing their capital structure to maximize returns and flexibility. This mindset shift—from static ownership to dynamic financial management—is what enables long-term success in the short-term rental industry.

Ultimately, the strategies outlined in this book are designed to empower you to take control of your financial future. By learning how to unlock and leverage the equity within your Airbnb properties, you gain access to a powerful toolset that can accelerate your growth, increase your income, and expand your opportunities. Whether your goal is to acquire more properties, diversify your portfolio, or achieve financial independence, refinancing and equity extraction provide the pathway to get there.

This is where your journey evolves from building income to building wealth. The properties you have worked hard to acquire are no longer just assets—they are stepping stones to something much greater. As you master the concepts in this book, you will begin to see opportunities where others see limitations, and you will develop the confidence to execute strategies that can transform your portfolio and your life.

Chapter 1

The Foundation of Airbnb Refinancing — Understanding the Opportunity

The journey into Airbnb mortgage loan refinancing begins with a fundamental shift in how you view real estate. Most people see a property as something static—a place to live, a rental to collect income from, or an asset that slowly appreciates over time. However, in the world of short-term rentals and advanced financing strategies, a property becomes something far more powerful. It becomes a dynamic financial instrument capable of generating income, creating equity, and funding future investments. This is the foundation upon which everything else in this book is built.

Airbnb properties operate differently from traditional real estate investments. Unlike long-term rentals, which provide steady but often limited income, short-term rentals offer the potential for significantly higher revenue through nightly pricing, dynamic demand, and premium guest experiences. This increased income potential changes the entire equation when it comes to financing and refinancing. Instead of relying solely on your personal income to qualify for loans, you can leverage the income generated by the property itself. This opens the door to a new class of financing options, particularly

DSCR loans, which evaluate the property's ability to cover its debt rather than your personal financial profile.

Refinancing, in its simplest form, is the process of replacing an existing loan with a new one. But in the context of Airbnb investing, refinancing becomes a strategic tool rather than a routine transaction. It allows you to unlock the equity you have built in your property, adjust your loan terms, and reposition your investment for future growth. This is where the concept of "working capital" begins to take shape. The equity in your property is not just a number—it is a resource that can be accessed and redeployed.

One of the most important concepts to understand is how equity is created. Equity grows in two primary ways: through appreciation and through loan paydown. Appreciation can occur naturally as the market increases in value, but in the Airbnb model, it is often driven by income performance. A well-managed short-term rental that generates strong revenue can justify a higher valuation, particularly when lenders consider income-based metrics. This means that your efforts to optimize your property—improving design, enhancing guest experience, and maximizing occupancy—directly contribute to your ability to refinance and extract equity. Another critical element is understanding loan-to-value ratio, or LTV. This metric determines how much of a property's value a lender is willing to finance. For investment properties, this is typically between 70% and 75%. The difference between the loan amount and the property's value represents your equity. When you refinance, you are essentially recalculating this relationship based on the current value of the property. If the value has increased, you may be able to access additional funds without selling the property.

However, refinancing is not just about accessing cash. It is also about improving your financial position. A rate-and-term refinance, for example, can reduce your interest rate, lower your monthly payments, and improve cash flow. This can make your investment more sustainable and resilient over time. On the other hand, a cash-out refinance allows you to access equity for reinvestment, enabling you to scale your portfolio. Understanding the difference between these strategies—and when to use each—is essential for building a successful Airbnb investment plan.

The opportunity within Airbnb refinancing lies in its ability to create a cycle of growth. Instead of saving for years to acquire another property, you can use the equity from your existing investments to fund new opportunities. This accelerates your progress and allows you to build a portfolio much faster than traditional methods would allow. This concept, often referred to as "equity recycling," is one of the most powerful tools available to real estate investors.

At the same time, it is important to recognize that this opportunity comes with responsibility. Leveraging equity increases your exposure to risk, and it requires careful planning and disciplined execution. Each refinance decision should be made with a clear understanding of its impact on cash flow, debt levels, and overall portfolio stability. The goal is not just to grow quickly, but to grow sustainably.

As you begin to explore Airbnb refinancing, you will also need to understand the role of lenders and loan products. Not all lenders are equipped to handle short-term rental income, and not all loan products are suitable for Airbnb properties. DSCR loans, portfolio loans, and certain non-QM products are often the most relevant options. Building relationships with lenders who understand this space can provide access to better terms and more flexibility.

Another key factor is documentation and presentation. Lenders need to see that your property is performing consistently and generating reliable income. This means maintaining accurate records, tracking your revenue, and presenting your property in the best possible light. The more organized and professional you are, the easier it becomes to secure favorable financing. Timing is also a critical component of the refinancing process. Refinancing too early may limit your ability to access equity, while waiting too long could expose you to market risks. Understanding when your property has reached its full potential—and when market conditions are favorable—can significantly impact your results. This requires a combination of data analysis, market awareness, and strategic thinking.

Ultimately, the foundation of Airbnb refinancing is about understanding how all these elements come together. It is about recognizing the potential within your properties and using that potential to create new opportunities. It is about moving beyond a passive approach to real estate and embracing a more dynamic, strategic mindset.

This chapter sets the stage for everything that follows. By understanding the fundamentals of Airbnb refinancing, you gain the tools and perspective needed to navigate more advanced strategies. You begin to see your properties not just as investments, but as building blocks in a larger system of wealth creation.

Real Life Math Example: Understanding Equity and Refinance Potential

Let's consider an investor named Sarah who purchases an Airbnb property for $400,000. She puts down 20%, which is

$80,000, and finances the remaining $320,000. She invests an additional $20,000 into furnishing and optimizing the property for short-term rental use, bringing her total investment to $100,000.

In the first year, Sarah's property generates an average monthly revenue of $6,000, or $72,000 annually. After expenses, her net operating income is $45,000 per year. This strong performance not only provides cash flow but also contributes to the property's value.

After one year, the property is appraised at $500,000 due to both market appreciation and its income performance. Sarah's loan balance has been reduced to $310,000. This means her total equity is now $190,000 ($500,000 minus $310,000).

Sarah decides to explore a cash-out refinance. The lender offers a maximum LTV of 75%, which means she can borrow up to $375,000 (75% of $500,000). After paying off her existing loan of $310,000, she is left with $65,000 in cash before closing costs. After deducting $5,000 in costs, she receives $60,000.

Now, Sarah has recovered a significant portion of her initial investment while still owning the property. Her new loan is $375,000, and her monthly payment increases slightly. However, because the property generates strong income, she continues to maintain positive cash flow. Sarah uses the $60,000 to invest in another property, either as a down payment or in combination with additional funds. This allows her to expand her portfolio without relying solely on new savings.

If Sarah repeats this process over time, each property can contribute to the acquisition of the next. For example, if her second property also appreciates and generates strong income, she can refinance again and access additional capital. Over several years, this creates a cycle of growth where her portfolio expands through the strategic use of equity.

Let's take the numbers further. Suppose Sarah acquires three properties over five years, each generating $2,500 per month in net income. Her total monthly income would be $7,500, or $90,000 annually. If each property is valued at $500,000, her total portfolio value is $1.5 million, with significant equity built over time.

This example illustrates the foundational concept of Airbnb refinancing. By understanding how equity is created and accessed, Sarah is able to transform a single investment into a growing portfolio. The key is not just the numbers, but the strategy behind them—using each property as a stepping stone to the next opportunity.

Chapter 2

Understanding Cash-Out Refinance for Airbnb Properties

Cash-out refinancing is one of the most powerful tools available to Airbnb investors who are serious about scaling their portfolios and accelerating wealth creation. At its core, a cash-out refinance allows you to replace your existing mortgage with a new, larger loan based on the current value of your property, while receiving the difference in cash. This strategy transforms your property from a static asset into a dynamic source of capital. Instead of waiting years to save for your next investment, you can leverage the appreciation and income performance of your Airbnb property to fund your next deal. This is how sophisticated investors grow quickly without relying on outside investors or excessive personal savings.

To fully understand how a cash-out refinance works, you must first understand the relationship between property value, loan-to-value ratio (LTV), and available equity. As your Airbnb property increases in value—either through market appreciation, property improvements, or increased income—your equity grows. Lenders typically allow you to borrow up to a certain percentage of that value, often between 70% and 75% for investment properties. The difference between your current loan balance and the new loan amount becomes the cash you can access. For Airbnb investors, this can be substantial, especially if the property has been optimized to generate strong short-term rental income.

One of the key advantages of Airbnb properties is their ability to produce higher income than traditional long-term rentals. This increased income can lead to higher valuations, particularly when lenders use DSCR-based underwriting. Unlike conventional loans that rely heavily on borrower income, DSCR loans focus on the property's ability to generate enough income to cover its debt obligations. If your Airbnb property consistently produces strong revenue, it may qualify for a higher valuation, which in turn increases the amount of equity you can extract through a cash-out refinance. This creates a powerful feedback loop where better property performance leads to more accessible capital.

However, cash-out refinancing is not simply about pulling out as much money as possible. Strategic investors approach this process with a clear plan for how the funds will be used. The goal is not just to access equity, but to redeploy it into opportunities that generate additional income and long-term value. This could include purchasing another Airbnb property, renovating an existing one to increase its nightly rate, or diversifying into different markets. Each decision should be guided by a clear investment strategy and a thorough understanding of risk and return.

Another important consideration is the impact of a cash-out refinance on your monthly cash flow. When you increase your loan balance, your monthly payment will typically increase as well. This means that your property must generate enough income to comfortably cover the new debt service while still providing positive cash flow. This is where careful analysis becomes critical. Investors must evaluate not only the potential benefits of accessing equity, but also the long-term sustainability of the new loan structure. A successful cash-out refinance should strengthen your financial position, not weaken it.

Timing also plays a crucial role in maximizing the benefits of a cash-out refinance. Refinancing too early, before the property has reached its full income potential or appreciated sufficiently, can limit the amount of equity you can access. On the other hand, waiting too long could expose you to market risks such as rising interest rates or declining property values. The ideal timing is when your property has demonstrated consistent income, achieved strong occupancy rates, and benefited from market appreciation. At this point, you are in the best position to secure favorable loan terms and maximize your cash-out proceeds. In addition to timing, lenders will evaluate several key factors when considering a cash-out refinance for an Airbnb property. These include the property's income history, occupancy rates, location, and overall market conditions. Properties in high-demand vacation markets with strong tourism trends are often viewed more favorably, as they are more likely to generate consistent income. Investors should be prepared to provide detailed documentation, including rental income reports, booking history, and expense statements. Presenting a well-documented and professionally managed property can significantly improve your chances of approval.

It is also important to understand the costs associated with a cash-out refinance. These can include appraisal fees, closing costs, lender fees, and potentially higher interest rates compared to rate-and-term refinances. While these costs can be significant, they should be viewed in the context of the overall investment strategy. If the funds obtained through the refinance are used to acquire additional income-producing assets, the long-term benefits can far outweigh the initial expenses. The key is to ensure that the return on the reinvested capital exceeds the cost of borrowing.

Risk management is another critical component of any cash-out refinance strategy. While leveraging equity can accelerate growth, it also increases exposure to market fluctuations and operational challenges. Investors must be prepared for scenarios such as lower-than-expected occupancy, seasonal fluctuations, or unexpected expenses. Maintaining adequate reserves and conservative financial projections can help mitigate these risks. The goal is to create a resilient portfolio that can withstand market volatility while continuing to generate consistent income.

As you continue to build your Airbnb portfolio, cash-out refinancing becomes more than just a financing tool—it becomes a core component of your overall strategy. By systematically extracting and redeploying equity, you can create a cycle of continuous growth. Each property contributes to the acquisition of the next, and over time, your portfolio expands at an accelerating pace. This is the essence of scaling in real estate, and it is made possible through the strategic use of leverage.

Ultimately, mastering cash-out refinancing requires a combination of financial knowledge, strategic planning, and disciplined execution. It is not a one-size-fits-all approach, and each investor must tailor their strategy to their specific goals, risk tolerance, and market conditions. However, for those who take the time to understand and apply these principles, the rewards can be substantial. Cash-out refinancing offers a pathway to faster growth, greater financial flexibility, and the ability to turn a single property into a thriving real estate portfolio.

Real Life Math Example: Cash-Out Refinance Strategy for an Airbnb Property

Imagine an investor named Daniel who purchased an Airbnb property in a high-demand vacation market for $400,000. He put down 20%, or $80,000, and financed the remaining $320,000 with a mortgage. Over the next two years, Daniel focused on optimizing the property for short-term rentals. He invested in high-quality furnishings, improved the property's design, and implemented dynamic pricing strategies to maximize occupancy and nightly rates. As a result, the property began generating strong income, averaging $6,500 per month in gross rental revenue.

At the same time, the property appreciated in value due to both market conditions and its strong income performance. After two years, a new appraisal valued the property at $550,000. Daniel's remaining loan balance had been paid down to $300,000. This means that his total equity in the property is now $250,000 ($550,000 value minus $300,000 loan balance). This equity represents an opportunity to access capital through a cash-out refinance.

Daniel approaches a lender who offers a DSCR cash-out refinance with a maximum loan-to-value ratio of 75%. Based on the new appraised value of $550,000, the maximum loan amount he can obtain is $412,500 (75% of $550,000). Since his current loan balance is $300,000, the difference between the new loan and the existing loan is $112,500. This is the amount of cash Daniel can receive at closing, before accounting for closing costs and fees.

After deducting approximately $10,000 in closing costs, Daniel walks away with roughly $102,500 in cash. Importantly, he still owns the property, which continues to generate income. His new loan balance is $412,500, and his monthly mortgage payment increases accordingly. However, because the property generates $6,500 per month in revenue, and his new monthly payment is approximately $3,200, he still maintains positive cash flow after expenses.

Daniel now uses the $102,500 to purchase a second Airbnb property. He finds a property priced at $450,000 and uses the funds for a down payment and initial setup costs. By repeating the same optimization strategies, he is able to generate strong income from the second property as well. Over time, this second property will also appreciate and build equity, creating another opportunity for refinancing and capital extraction.

If Daniel continues this process, he can build a portfolio of multiple properties using the equity from his initial investment. For example, after another two to three years, his second property may also appreciate significantly, allowing him to perform another cash-out refinance. This creates a cycle where each property contributes to the acquisition of the next, accelerating portfolio growth.

Let's take the math one step further. Suppose Daniel repeats this process three times over a period of six to eight years. Starting with one property and using cash-out refinancing, he acquires a total of four properties. Each property generates an average net cash flow of $2,000 per month after expenses. This results in a total monthly cash flow of $8,000 across the portfolio, or $96,000 per year.

In addition to cash flow, Daniel has also built significant equity across all properties. If each property is now valued at an average of $600,000, his total portfolio value is $2.4 million. Even after accounting for loan balances, he may have over $800,000 in equity. This equity can be used for further investments, diversification, or long-term wealth preservation.

This example illustrates the power of cash-out refinancing when applied strategically. By leveraging appreciation and income, Daniel was able to transform a single property into a multi-property portfolio generating substantial income and equity. The key to his success was not just accessing equity, but using it wisely to acquire additional income-producing assets.

Chapter 3

The BRRRR Strategy for Airbnb Properties

The BRRRR strategy—Buy, Rehab, Rent, Refinance, Repeat—has long been one of the most powerful methods for building wealth in real estate, but its evolution into the Airbnb and short-term rental space has created an even more dynamic and accelerated path to scaling a portfolio. In traditional real estate investing, the BRRRR method focuses on purchasing undervalued long-term rental properties, improving them, renting them out, refinancing to recover capital, and repeating the process. However, when applied to Airbnb properties, this strategy takes on a new level of profitability and speed because short-term rentals can generate significantly higher income, which directly impacts valuation and refinance potential.

The first step, "Buy," is critical because it sets the foundation for the entire strategy. Airbnb investors must identify properties with strong short-term rental potential, not just based on purchase price but on location, demand, and revenue potential. Unlike traditional rentals, where long-term lease rates are relatively stable and predictable, Airbnb income can vary significantly depending on factors such as tourism demand, seasonality, proximity to attractions, and property uniqueness. This means that a property that may not appear attractive as a long-term rental could be extremely profitable as a short-term rental. Successful investors learn to analyze markets through an Airbnb lens, focusing on average daily rates, occupancy trends, and competition rather than just comparable sales.

The second step, "Rehab," is where value is actively created. In the Airbnb model, rehabilitation goes beyond basic repairs and renovations. It includes designing the property to stand out in the marketplace, creating an experience that attracts guests, and optimizing the layout and amenities for maximum appeal. This could involve modernizing the interior, adding unique design elements, upgrading furnishings, or even incorporating features like hot tubs, game rooms, or outdoor entertainment spaces. The goal is not just to increase the property's physical value, but to enhance its income-generating potential. A well-designed Airbnb property can command higher nightly rates and achieve better occupancy, which ultimately drives higher overall revenue.

The "Rent" phase in the Airbnb BRRRR strategy is where the true power of short-term rentals becomes evident. Instead of securing a long-term tenant at a fixed monthly rate, the property is listed on platforms like Airbnb and begins generating income on a nightly basis. This allows investors to capitalize on peak seasons, adjust pricing dynamically, and maximize revenue. A properly managed Airbnb property can often generate two to three times the income of a comparable long-term rental. This increased income is not only beneficial for cash flow, but it also plays a crucial role in the next step of the strategy: refinancing.

Refinancing in the Airbnb BRRRR strategy is fundamentally different from traditional BRRRR because of the way lenders evaluate income. In many cases, DSCR loans are used, which focus on the property's ability to generate income rather than the borrower's personal income. If the Airbnb property demonstrates strong and consistent revenue, it may qualify for a higher valuation based on its income performance. This can allow investors to recover a significant portion, or even all, of their initial investment. The refinance step effectively replenishes the capital used to acquire and improve the property, making it available for the next investment.

The final step, "Repeat," is where the strategy compounds. By continuously reinvesting the capital recovered through refinancing, investors can acquire additional properties and scale their portfolios. Each successful cycle increases both income and equity, creating a snowball effect that accelerates growth. Over time, this process can transform a single property into a diversified portfolio of income-producing assets. The key to success lies in executing each step effectively and maintaining a disciplined approach to risk management and financial planning.

One of the most significant advantages of applying the BRRRR strategy to Airbnb properties is the potential for forced appreciation. In traditional real estate, appreciation is often dependent on market conditions. However, with Airbnb properties, investors can actively influence value by increasing income. Since income is a major factor in valuation for DSCR loans and certain appraisal methods, improving the property's performance can directly increase its appraised value. This means that investors are not solely reliant on market appreciation—they can create value through operational excellence.

However, the Airbnb BRRRR strategy also comes with unique challenges. Short-term rental markets can be more volatile than long-term rental markets, with fluctuations in demand due to seasonality, economic conditions, and local regulations. Investors must be prepared to adapt to these changes and implement strategies to maintain consistent occupancy and revenue. This may include diversifying marketing channels, adjusting pricing strategies, or targeting different types of guests. Additionally, understanding local regulations and zoning laws is critical, as some areas have restrictions on short-term rentals that can impact profitability. Financing is another important consideration in the Airbnb BRRRR strategy. Not all lenders are comfortable with short-term rental income, and loan terms can vary significantly. Investors must identify lenders who understand the Airbnb model and offer products such as DSCR loans or other non-QM options. Building relationships with these lenders and understanding their requirements can streamline the refinancing process and improve the likelihood of approval. Preparation and documentation are key, as lenders will often require detailed income reports and performance data.

Risk management remains a central theme throughout the BRRRR process. While the strategy offers significant potential for growth, it also involves leveraging debt and reinvesting capital, which can increase exposure to market fluctuations. Investors must ensure that each deal is financially sound, with conservative projections and adequate reserves. The goal is to build a portfolio that is not only profitable but also resilient. This means avoiding over-leveraging and maintaining a balance between growth and stability.

As you master the Airbnb BRRRR strategy, you begin to shift from being a property owner to being a portfolio builder. Each property becomes a stepping stone to the next, and your focus expands from individual deals to overall portfolio performance. This mindset is essential for long-term success, as it allows you to make strategic decisions that align with your broader financial goals. The BRRRR strategy is not just about acquiring properties—it is about creating a system for continuous growth and wealth creation.

Ultimately, the Airbnb BRRRR strategy represents one of the most efficient ways to scale a real estate portfolio using limited initial capital. By combining the principles of value creation, income optimization, and strategic refinancing, investors can achieve exponential growth over time. The key is to approach each step with intention, discipline, and a clear understanding of the underlying financial principles. When executed correctly, this strategy can transform your Airbnb investments into a powerful engine for long-term wealth.

Real Life Math Example: Applying the Airbnb BRRRR Strategy

Consider an investor named Sofia who identifies a property in a growing vacation market priced at $350,000. The property is outdated but structurally sound, making it an ideal candidate for the BRRRR strategy. Sofia negotiates the purchase and puts down 20%, or $70,000, while financing the remaining $280,000. She allocates an additional $30,000 for renovations, bringing her total initial investment to $100,000. During the rehab phase, Sofia focuses on transforming the property into a high-performing Airbnb. She upgrades the kitchen and bathrooms, adds modern furnishings, and creates a unique design theme that appeals to travelers. She also installs a hot tub and enhances the outdoor space to increase the property's appeal. After completing the renovations, the property is listed on Airbnb and quickly gains traction due to its attractive design and competitive pricing.

In the first year of operation, Sofia's property generates an average monthly revenue of $7,000, or $84,000 annually. After accounting for expenses such as cleaning, utilities, maintenance, and property management, her net operating income is approximately $50,000 per year. This strong income performance significantly increases the property's value when evaluated by a lender using a DSCR approach.

After 12 months of consistent income, Sofia orders a new appraisal. Due to both the renovations and the strong rental performance, the property is now valued at $500,000. This represents a substantial increase from the original purchase price of $350,000. Sofia's remaining loan balance is approximately $270,000, as she has made some principal payments during the year.

Sofia approaches a lender offering a DSCR cash-out refinance with a maximum loan-to-value ratio of 75%. Based on the new appraised value of $500,000, she qualifies for a new loan of $375,000. After paying off the existing loan balance of $270,000, she is left with $105,000 in cash-out proceeds before closing costs. After deducting approximately $8,000 in fees, Sofia receives around $97,000 in usable capital.

At this point, Sofia has nearly recovered her entire initial investment of $100,000 while still owning the property. The property continues to generate strong cash flow, even with the new loan payment. Her monthly mortgage payment increases, but the property still produces positive net income due to its high revenue.

Sofia then uses the $97,000 to acquire a second property using the same BRRRR strategy. She repeats the process: purchasing a property with potential, renovating it to maximize Airbnb income, stabilizing its performance, and refinancing to recover her capital. Over time, each cycle adds another property to her portfolio while recycling the same initial investment.

If Sofia repeats this process three times over a five-year period, she could potentially own four properties, each generating significant cash flow. Assuming each property produces a net monthly income of $2,500 after expenses, her total monthly income would be $10,000, or $120,000 per year. Additionally, each property may have appreciated in value, further increasing her equity. Let's assume that after five years, each property is valued at an average of $550,000. With four properties, Sofia's total portfolio value is $2.2 million. Even if her total loan balances across all properties amount to $1.5 million, she still holds $700,000 in equity. This equity can be accessed through future refinancing or used as leverage for larger investments.

This example demonstrates how the Airbnb BRRRR strategy allows investors to scale rapidly by recycling capital and leveraging income performance. Sofia started with $100,000 and, through strategic execution, transformed it into a multi-property portfolio generating substantial income and equity. The key to her success was not just finding good deals, but maximizing the potential of each property and using refinancing to fuel continued growth.

Chapter 4

Equity Recycling and Portfolio Scaling

Equity recycling is one of the most powerful and misunderstood strategies in real estate investing, especially within the Airbnb and short-term rental space. While many investors focus on acquiring properties and generating monthly cash flow, the most successful portfolio builders understand that the real wealth is created through the strategic use of equity. Equity is not just a number on paper—it is a financial resource that, when accessed and redeployed correctly, can accelerate growth far beyond what is possible with traditional savings alone. In the context of Airbnb investing, where properties can generate strong income and appreciate rapidly, equity recycling becomes a core strategy for scaling quickly and efficiently.

At its foundation, equity recycling involves extracting equity from one property—typically through a cash-out refinance or a line of credit—and using those funds to acquire additional income-producing assets. Instead of allowing equity to remain idle within a property, it is actively put to work, generating new income streams and increasing overall portfolio value. This creates a compounding effect, where each property contributes to the growth of the next. Over time, this cycle can lead to exponential expansion, transforming a small portfolio into a large and diversified real estate business.

One of the key reasons equity recycling is so effective in Airbnb investing is the unique income profile of short-term rentals. Unlike long-term rentals, which generate relatively fixed monthly income, Airbnb properties have the potential to produce significantly higher revenue through dynamic pricing, seasonal demand, and premium guest experiences. This higher income can lead to higher property valuations, particularly when lenders use DSCR-based underwriting. As a result, Airbnb investors often have more equity to access compared to traditional rental investors, making equity recycling even more impactful.

However, successful equity recycling requires more than just accessing capital—it requires strategic planning and disciplined execution. Each decision must be evaluated in terms of both risk and return. Extracting equity increases leverage, which can amplify both gains and losses. Investors must ensure that each new acquisition is financially sound and contributes positively to the overall portfolio. This means analyzing deals carefully, maintaining conservative assumptions, and avoiding the temptation to overextend. Another critical aspect of equity recycling is understanding the concept of velocity of capital. This refers to how quickly you can deploy, recover, and redeploy your capital. The faster you can complete this cycle, the faster your portfolio grows. In the Airbnb model, this is often achieved through a combination of property optimization and strategic refinancing. By quickly stabilizing a property's income and increasing its value, investors can refinance sooner and access capital for the next deal. This creates a continuous loop of growth that can significantly accelerate portfolio expansion.

Portfolio scaling through equity recycling also requires a shift in mindset: Instead of viewing each property as an isolated investment, you begin to see your portfolio as an interconnected system. Each property plays a role in the overall strategy, contributing income, equity, and growth potential. Decisions are made not just based on individual property performance, but on how they impact the portfolio as a whole. This holistic approach allows investors to optimize their capital allocation and maximize long-term returns.

Diversification is another important consideration when scaling a portfolio through equity recycling. While it may be tempting to focus on a single market or property type, spreading investments across different locations and asset classes can reduce risk and increase stability. For example, an investor might combine urban Airbnb properties with vacation rentals in tourist destinations, balancing seasonal fluctuations and market dynamics. Diversification also provides more opportunities for refinancing and equity extraction, as different markets may appreciate at different rates.

Financing plays a central role in equity recycling and portfolio scaling. Investors must develop a deep understanding of available loan products, including DSCR loans, portfolio loans, and lines of credit. Each financing option has its own advantages and limitations, and choosing the right one depends on your specific goals and circumstances. Building relationships with lenders who understand the Airbnb model can provide access to more flexible and competitive financing options, making it easier to execute your strategy.

Cash flow management is equally important when scaling a portfolio. As you acquire more properties and increase leverage, maintaining positive cash flow becomes essential for sustainability. Each property should generate enough income to cover its expenses and contribute to overall portfolio performance. This requires careful budgeting, efficient property management, and ongoing optimization. Investors must also maintain adequate reserves to handle unexpected expenses and market fluctuations, ensuring that their portfolio remains resilient.

Technology and data play a significant role in modern Airbnb investing and equity recycling. Tools that provide insights into pricing, occupancy trends, and market demand can help investors make informed decisions and optimize property performance. By leveraging data, investors can identify opportunities to increase revenue, improve efficiency, and enhance guest experiences. This not only boosts cash flow but also strengthens the property's valuation, creating more opportunities for equity extraction.

Another key element of equity recycling is exit strategy planning. While the primary goal may be to hold and scale properties, investors should also consider potential exit options. This could include selling properties to realize gains, refinancing into long-term debt for stability, or transitioning to different investment strategies. Having a clear exit plan provides flexibility and ensures that you can adapt to changing market conditions. It also allows you to capture value at the right time and reinvest in new opportunities.

Risk management becomes increasingly important as your portfolio grows. Higher leverage and multiple properties introduce additional complexities and potential vulnerabilities. Investors must be proactive in identifying and mitigating risks, including market downturns, regulatory changes, and operational challenges. This involves maintaining strong financial discipline, staying informed about market trends, and continuously evaluating portfolio performance. The goal is to build a portfolio that can withstand uncertainty while continuing to generate consistent returns.

As you scale your Airbnb portfolio through equity recycling, you begin to unlock new levels of financial freedom and opportunity. The income generated from your properties can support your lifestyle, while the equity provides a foundation for future growth. Over time, your portfolio becomes a powerful asset that can be leveraged for various purposes, including further investments, business ventures, or long-term wealth preservation. This is the true power of equity recycling—it transforms real estate from a passive investment into an active engine for wealth creation.

Ultimately, equity recycling is not just a strategy—it is a philosophy of investing. It requires a proactive approach, a willingness to take calculated risks, and a commitment to continuous improvement. By mastering this approach, you can move beyond the limitations of traditional investing and create a scalable, self-sustaining portfolio. Each property becomes a building block, each refinance a catalyst, and each reinvestment a step toward greater financial independence.

This is how portfolios are built, and this is how wealth is created in the modern Airbnb economy.

Real Life Math Example: Scaling an Airbnb Portfolio Through Equity Recycling

Let's consider an investor named Marcus who begins his Airbnb journey with a single property. He purchases a property for $300,000, putting down 20%, or $60,000, and financing the remaining $240,000. He invests an additional $20,000 into furnishing and optimizing the property for short-term rental use, bringing his total initial investment to $80,000. After launching the property on Airbnb, Marcus generates an average monthly revenue of $5,500, or $66,000 annually. After expenses, his net operating income is approximately $40,000 per year.

Over the next two years, the property appreciates in value due to both market conditions and its strong income performance. A new appraisal values the property at $420,000. Marcus's remaining loan balance is approximately $230,000. This means he now has $190,000 in equity. He decides to perform a cash-out refinance at 75% LTV, allowing him to take out a new loan of $315,000. After paying off the existing loan, he receives $85,000 in cash after closing costs.

Marcus uses the $85,000 to acquire a second Airbnb property priced at $350,000. He follows a similar strategy, investing in improvements and optimizing the property for short-term rental income. Within a year, the second property generates $6,000 per month in revenue, or $72,000 annually, with a net operating income of $45,000. The property appreciates to $460,000, and Marcus performs another cash-out refinance, extracting approximately $90,000 in equity.

Now, Marcus owns two properties and has recovered most of his initial capital. He uses the $90,000 to purchase a third property, continuing the cycle. Each property adds to his total income and equity, creating a compounding effect. After five years, Marcus owns four Airbnb properties, each generating an average net income of $2,500 per month. His total monthly income is now $10,000, or $120,000 annually.

Let's break down the portfolio value. If each property is valued at an average of $450,000, the total portfolio value is $1.8 million. Assuming total loan balances of $1.2 million, Marcus has $600,000 in equity. This equity can be used for further investments or as a financial cushion. Additionally, the portfolio generates consistent cash flow, providing financial stability and flexibility.

Marcus's success is driven by his ability to recycle equity

efficiently. Instead of saving for each new property, he uses the equity from existing properties to fund new acquisitions. This allows him to scale much faster than traditional investors. By focusing on high-performing Airbnb properties and leveraging DSCR-based refinancing, he maximizes both income and valuation.

If Marcus continues this strategy for another five years, he could potentially double his portfolio again, reaching eight properties. Assuming similar performance, his monthly income could exceed $20,000, and his portfolio value could surpass $3 million. This demonstrates the exponential potential of equity recycling when applied consistently and strategically.

This example highlights the importance of discipline and planning in equity recycling. Marcus carefully evaluates each deal, maintains positive cash flow, and avoids over-leveraging. He also reinvests his capital into properties with strong income potential, ensuring that each new acquisition contributes to the overall portfolio. By doing so, he creates a sustainable growth model that can adapt to changing market conditions.

In conclusion, equity recycling is a powerful strategy that enables investors to scale their Airbnb portfolios rapidly and efficiently. By leveraging the equity in existing properties and reinvesting it into new opportunities, investors can achieve exponential growth and build substantial wealth over time. The key is to approach each step with a clear strategy, disciplined execution, and a focus on long-term success.

Chapter 5

Rate-and-Term Refinance Strategies to Improve Cash Flow

While cash-out refinancing often gets the most attention due to its ability to unlock capital, the rate-and-term refinance is one of the most underrated and strategically powerful tools available to Airbnb investors. Unlike a cash-out refinance, which focuses on extracting equity, a rate-and-term refinance is designed to improve the terms of your existing loan—typically by lowering the interest rate, adjusting the loan term, or both. For investors focused on long-term stability, consistent cash flow, and risk reduction, this strategy can significantly enhance portfolio performance without increasing leverage.

At its core, a rate-and-term refinance replaces your existing mortgage with a new loan that has more favorable terms. This could mean securing a lower interest rate, extending the loan term to reduce monthly payments, or transitioning from an adjustable-rate mortgage to a fixed-rate structure. In the context of Airbnb investing, where income can fluctuate based on seasonality and market conditions, improving cash flow through lower monthly payments can provide a crucial buffer against volatility. This makes the rate-and-term refinance an essential tool for maintaining financial stability as your portfolio grows.

One of the primary benefits of a rate-and-term refinance is the ability to reduce your monthly mortgage payment. Even a small decrease in interest rate can result in significant savings over time. For example, reducing your interest rate from 7.5% to 6.25% on a large loan can lower your monthly payment by hundreds of dollars. When multiplied across multiple properties, these savings can add up to thousands of dollars per month. This increased cash flow can be reinvested into property improvements, marketing efforts, or reserve funds, all of which contribute to stronger long-term performance.

Another advantage of this strategy is improved predictability. Many Airbnb investors initially use adjustable-rate loans or short-term financing to acquire properties quickly. While these options can be effective in the early stages, they often come with interest rate risk. A rate-and-term refinance allows investors to transition into fixed-rate loans, locking in predictable payments over the long term. This stability is particularly valuable in uncertain economic environments, where rising interest rates can significantly impact profitability.

In addition to lowering payments and improving predictability, a rate-and-term refinance can also enhance your property's debt service coverage ratio (DSCR). Since DSCR is calculated by dividing the property's income by its debt obligations, reducing your monthly payment directly improves this ratio. A stronger DSCR not only increases your financial safety margin but can also make it easier to qualify for additional financing in the future. Lenders view properties with higher DSCRs as lower risk, which can lead to better loan terms and more favorable approval conditions.

Timing is a critical factor when considering a rate-and-term refinance. Interest rates fluctuate based on broader economic conditions, and identifying the right moment to refinance can significantly impact your results. Investors should monitor market trends and be prepared to act when rates drop or when their property's performance improves. Additionally, refinancing after increasing a property's income—through better management, renovations, or pricing strategies—can further enhance the benefits by improving loan eligibility and terms.

It is also important to consider the costs associated with refinancing. These may include appraisal fees, closing costs, and lender fees. While these expenses can be substantial, they should be evaluated in the context of long-term savings. In many cases, the reduction in monthly payments and interest costs can offset the initial expenses within a relatively short period. Investors often calculate a "break-even point" to determine how long it will take for the savings to exceed the costs. This analysis helps ensure that the refinance aligns with their financial goals.

Another strategic use of rate-and-term refinancing is to extend the loan term. By moving from a 20-year loan to a 30-year loan, for example, investors can significantly reduce their monthly payments. While this may increase the total interest paid over the life of the loan, it can free up cash flow in the short term, which can be used for other investments or operational needs. This trade-off between short-term cash flow and long-term cost must be carefully evaluated based on individual goals and circumstances.

Rate-and-term refinancing can also be used to reposition a property within your portfolio. For example, an investor may initially acquire a property using a higher-cost loan due to limited options or time constraints. Once the property is stabilized and generating consistent income, they can refinance into a more favorable loan, improving both cash flow and overall returns. This approach allows investors to act quickly on opportunities while still optimizing their financing over time.

As your Airbnb portfolio grows, the cumulative impact of rate-and-term refinancing becomes increasingly significant. Each property that benefits from improved loan terms contributes to overall portfolio stability and profitability. Over time, these incremental improvements can result in substantial gains, both in terms of cash flow and long-term wealth. This is particularly important for investors who aim to hold properties for extended periods and build sustainable income streams.

Risk management is another key consideration. By reducing monthly payments and securing fixed-rate financing, investors can mitigate the impact of market fluctuations and unexpected expenses. This creates a more resilient portfolio that can withstand economic downturns and changes in demand. Maintaining strong cash flow and manageable debt levels ensures that you can continue operating effectively, even in challenging conditions.

Ultimately, the rate-and-term refinance is about optimization rather than expansion. It complements other strategies, such as cash-out refinancing and equity recycling, by strengthening the foundation of your portfolio. While it may not provide immediate access to large amounts of capital, it enhances your financial position and creates the stability needed for long-term success. By incorporating this strategy into your overall plan, you can achieve a balanced approach to growth and sustainability.

Real Life Math Example: Improving Cash Flow with a Rate-and-Term Refinance

Consider an investor named Elena who owns an Airbnb property valued at $500,000. She originally financed the property with a loan of $400,000 at an interest rate of 7.5% on a 30-year term. Her monthly mortgage payment, including principal and interest, is approximately $2,800. The property generates an average monthly revenue of $6,000, with net operating income of $4,000 after expenses.

While the property is profitable, Elena wants to improve her cash flow and reduce her financial risk. After monitoring interest rates, she identifies an opportunity to refinance at a lower rate of 6.25%. She decides to pursue a rate-and-term refinance, replacing her existing loan with a new loan of $395,000 (accounting for some principal reduction) at the lower interest rate.

With the new loan terms, Elena's monthly mortgage payment decreases to approximately $2,430. This results in a monthly savings of $370. Over the course of a year, this translates to $4,440 in additional cash flow. Over five years, the savings amount to $22,200, not including the potential benefits of reinvesting this cash flow. Let's analyze the impact on her DSCR. Before refinancing, her DSCR was calculated as $4,000 divided by $2,800, which equals approximately 1.43. After refinancing, her DSCR improves to $4,000 divided by $2,430, or approximately 1.65. This improvement not only increases her financial safety margin but also strengthens her position for future financing opportunities.

Elena incurs $8,000 in closing costs for the refinance. To determine her break-even point, she divides the total costs by her monthly savings of $370. This results in a break-even period of approximately 22 months. After this point, all additional savings contribute directly to her profit.

Now consider the long-term impact. If Elena holds the property for 10 years, her total savings from the lower interest rate could exceed $40,000. This additional cash flow can be used to fund property improvements, build reserves, or invest in new opportunities. By improving her financial position, she creates more flexibility and reduces her overall risk.

If Elena owns multiple properties and applies the same strategy to each one, the cumulative effect becomes even more significant. For example, if she has four properties and saves an average of $350 per month on each, her total monthly savings would be $1,400, or $16,800 per year. Over a decade, this could result in over $150,000 in additional cash flow.

This example demonstrates how a rate-and-term refinance can enhance both short-term cash flow and long-term profitability. By securing better loan terms, Elena improves her financial stability and positions herself for continued growth. While the strategy may not provide immediate access to capital like a cash-out refinance, its impact on cash flow and risk management makes it an essential component of a successful Airbnb investment strategy.

Chapter 6

Timing the Refinance — When to Pull Equity and When to Wait

One of the most critical—and often overlooked—skills in Airbnb investing is mastering the timing of your refinance. Knowing how to refinance is important, but knowing when to refinance is what separates experienced investors from those who leave money on the table or take unnecessary risks. In the world of short-term rentals, where income, property values, and market conditions can shift quickly, timing becomes a strategic decision that directly impacts how much equity you can access, how favorable your loan terms will be, and how sustainable your portfolio remains over time.

At its core, refinancing is a snapshot decision based on three primary variables: property value, property income, and market conditions. These three factors are constantly evolving, and your ability to align them at the right moment determines the effectiveness of your refinance. If you refinance too early, you may not capture the full appreciation or income potential of the property. If you wait too long, you may face rising interest rates, declining demand, or changes in lending guidelines that reduce your options. The goal is to identify the optimal window where your property is performing at a high level and lending conditions are favorable.

One of the first indicators that it may be time to refinance is property appreciation. In the Airbnb model, appreciation can occur not only through general market growth but also through forced appreciation driven by increased income. As your property becomes more profitable—through higher occupancy rates, better reviews, improved amenities, and optimized pricing—it may justify a higher valuation. This is especially relevant when lenders use income-based approaches such as DSCR. Monitoring comparable sales, market trends, and appraisal data helps you determine whether your property has reached a value level that makes refinancing worthwhile.

Income stabilization is another key factor. Lenders want to see consistent and reliable income before approving a refinance, particularly for Airbnb properties. This typically means having several months—often 6 to 12 months—of documented rental history showing stable or growing revenue. If your property is newly listed or still in the optimization phase, refinancing too soon could result in a lower valuation or less favorable terms. On the other hand, once your property demonstrates consistent performance, it becomes a strong candidate for refinancing.

Interest rates play a significant role in refinance timing as well. Even if your property has appreciated and is generating strong income, high interest rates can reduce the benefits of refinancing. For example, pulling out equity at a higher rate may increase your monthly payments to a level that reduces or eliminates cash flow. This is why many investors monitor interest rate trends and wait for favorable conditions before refinancing. In some cases, it may be better to delay a refinance until rates improve, even if the property is otherwise ready.

Another important consideration is your overall investment strategy. The timing of a refinance should align with your broader goals, whether that is rapid portfolio expansion, cash flow optimization, or long-term stability. For example, an investor focused on scaling quickly may choose to refinance as soon as the property qualifies, even if conditions are not perfect, in order to access capital for new acquisitions. In contrast, an investor prioritizing stability may wait for the best possible terms before refinancing, ensuring that each move strengthens their financial position.

Market cycles also influence refinance timing. Real estate markets go through periods of growth, stability, and decline, and understanding where you are in the cycle can help inform your decisions. Refinancing during a strong market, when property values are high and demand is strong, can maximize the amount of equity you can extract. Conversely, attempting to refinance during a downturn may result in lower valuations and more restrictive lending conditions. Staying informed about local and national market trends allows you to anticipate changes and act proactively.

Liquidity and reserves should also be factored into your timing decisions. While refinancing can provide access to capital, it should not be your only source of liquidity. Investors should maintain sufficient reserves to cover expenses, vacancies, and unexpected events. Refinancing purely out of necessity, without a strategic plan, can lead to unfavorable outcomes. Instead, it should be part of a deliberate strategy to enhance your portfolio and create new opportunities.

Another subtle but important factor is property seasoning. Many lenders require a certain period of ownership before allowing a refinance, particularly for cash-out transactions. This seasoning period can range from six months to a year, depending on the loan product and lender guidelines. Understanding these requirements in advance helps you plan your timeline and avoid delays. It also reinforces the importance of optimizing your property's performance during the initial ownership period.

Tax considerations can also influence refinance timing. While refinancing itself is generally not a taxable event, the use of funds and the structure of your financing can have tax implications. Investors should consider how refinancing fits into their overall financial and tax strategy, particularly if they plan to reinvest the proceeds or use them for other purposes. Consulting with a tax professional can provide valuable insights and help ensure that your decisions align with your long-term goals.

As your portfolio grows, timing becomes even more important because each refinance decision affects not just one property, but the entire portfolio. A well-timed refinance can unlock capital, improve cash flow, and create new opportunities, while a poorly timed one can strain your finances and limit your flexibility. This is why experienced investors approach refinancing with a strategic mindset, carefully evaluating all relevant factors before making a decision.

Ultimately, mastering the timing of your refinance is about developing awareness and discipline. It requires staying informed about market conditions, monitoring your property's performance, and aligning your actions with your long-term strategy. By doing so, you can maximize the benefits of refinancing while minimizing risks, creating a strong foundation for continued growth and success in the Airbnb investment space.

Real Life Math Example: Timing a Cash-Out Refinance for Maximum Benefit

Consider an investor named Kevin who purchases an Airbnb property for $450,000 with a 20% down payment of $90,000. He finances the remaining $360,000 with a loan at 7% interest. After acquiring the property, Kevin invests $25,000 into renovations and furnishings, bringing his total investment to $115,000. He then launches the property as a short-term rental.

In the first six months, the property generates an average monthly revenue of $5,000. While this is a solid start, Kevin continues to optimize the listing by improving photos, adjusting pricing, and enhancing the guest experience. Over the next six months, his average monthly revenue increases to $6,500. By the end of the first year, the property has a strong track record of consistent income.

At this point, Kevin considers refinancing. However, he evaluates the situation carefully. The property has appreciated to $500,000, and his loan balance is approximately $350,000. If he refinances at 75% LTV, he could access a loan of $375,000, resulting in $25,000 in cash-out proceeds before costs. After closing costs, this amount would be even lower. Kevin decides that this is not an optimal time to refinance because the equity extraction is minimal. Instead, Kevin waits another year while continuing to optimize the property. By year two, the property generates $7,500 per month in revenue, and the market has appreciated further. A new appraisal values the property at $575,000. His loan balance has been reduced to $340,000. Now, at 75% LTV, he qualifies for a loan of $431,250. After paying off the existing loan, he can access $91,250 in cash before closing costs.

Let's compare the two scenarios. Refinancing at year one would have yielded approximately $20,000 after costs, while refinancing at year two yields approximately $85,000 after costs. By waiting and allowing both income and property value to increase, Kevin gains an additional $65,000 in usable capital. This demonstrates the importance of timing and patience in maximizing refinance benefits.

Now consider the impact on cash flow. Kevin's new loan of $431,250 comes with a monthly payment of approximately $3,300. With monthly revenue of $7,500 and net operating income of $5,000, he still maintains a strong positive cash flow. The increased loan balance is supported by the property's improved performance, ensuring that the refinance strengthens rather than weakens his financial position.

Kevin uses the $85,000 to acquire a second Airbnb property, continuing his growth strategy. By timing his refinance correctly, he maximizes the amount of capital available for reinvestment, accelerating his portfolio expansion.

If Kevin had rushed into refinancing earlier, he would have limited his ability to scale. By waiting for the right combination of income growth, property appreciation, and favorable conditions, he was able to significantly increase his return on investment. This example highlights how timing is not just a minor detail, but a critical component of a successful Airbnb refinance strategy.

Over time, Kevin applies this approach to each property in his portfolio, carefully evaluating when to refinance based on performance and market conditions. This disciplined strategy allows him to grow efficiently while maintaining strong cash flow and financial stability.

Chapter 7

Managing Risk When Leveraging Equity in Airbnb Investments

As you progress deeper into Airbnb investing and begin using refinancing and equity extraction as tools for scaling, one principle becomes absolutely critical: risk management. While leverage is what allows investors to grow quickly and build large portfolios, it is also what can create vulnerability if not handled correctly. The same strategies that can accelerate wealth—cash-out refinancing, equity recycling, and BRRRR—can also amplify losses if income drops, expenses rise, or market conditions shift. This chapter is focused on helping you understand how to use leverage intelligently so that you can grow aggressively while protecting your downside.

Leverage, by definition, means using borrowed money to increase your investment capacity. In real estate, this is what allows you to control large assets with relatively small amounts of your own capital. In Airbnb investing, leverage becomes even more powerful because properties can generate higher income than traditional rentals. However, this increased income often comes with increased variability. Unlike long-term leases, short-term rental income can fluctuate due to seasonality, competition, economic conditions, and changes in travel patterns. This means that your ability to manage risk is directly tied to your ability to handle variability in income.

The first and most important principle of risk management is maintaining strong cash flow margins. It is not enough for a property to simply break even or produce minimal profit. You need a cushion—a buffer that allows the property to remain profitable even if revenue declines temporarily. This means underwriting deals conservatively, using realistic occupancy assumptions, and accounting for all expenses, including maintenance, cleaning, utilities, management, and reserves. A property that looks profitable on paper under ideal conditions may become a liability if those conditions change.

Another key concept is debt service coverage ratio (DSCR), which measures how well a property's income covers its debt obligations. A DSCR above 1.0 means the property generates enough income to cover its mortgage, while a higher DSCR indicates a stronger safety margin. Many experienced investors aim for a DSCR of 1.3 to 1.5 or higher to ensure that they can handle fluctuations in income. When refinancing or taking on additional debt, maintaining a strong DSCR is essential for both lender approval and long-term sustainability.

Reserves are another critical component of risk management. As you increase leverage and acquire more properties, you must also increase your financial reserves. These reserves act as a safety net, allowing you to cover expenses during periods of lower occupancy or unexpected costs. A common guideline is to maintain at least three to six months of operating expenses for each property, though more conservative investors may hold even larger reserves. Having adequate reserves provides peace of mind and allows you to make decisions from a position of strength rather than desperation.

Diversification also plays a major role in managing risk. Relying on a single property or a single market exposes you to concentrated risk. If that market experiences a downturn or regulatory changes, your entire investment could be affected. By spreading your investments across different locations and property types, you reduce the impact of any single event. For example, combining urban properties with vacation destinations can help balance seasonal fluctuations and demand cycles.

Interest rate risk is another factor that must be carefully managed. Many investors use adjustable-rate loans or refinance into higher balances, which can increase exposure to rising interest rates. Locking in fixed rates when possible can provide stability and protect against future increases.

Additionally, understanding how changes in interest rates affect your monthly payments and overall cash flow is essential when making refinancing decisions.

Operational risk is particularly relevant in Airbnb investing. Unlike long-term rentals, short-term rentals require active management, including guest communication, cleaning coordination, maintenance, and marketing. Poor management can lead to negative reviews, lower occupancy, and reduced income. Implementing systems, hiring reliable vendors, and using technology to streamline operations can help mitigate these risks and ensure consistent performance.

Regulatory risk is another unique challenge in the Airbnb space. Local governments may impose restrictions on short-term rentals, including licensing requirements, occupancy limits, or outright bans in certain areas. Investors must stay informed about local regulations and choose markets that are favorable to Airbnb operations. This includes understanding zoning laws, HOA rules, and any potential changes that could impact your ability to operate.

As your portfolio grows, risk management becomes more complex because each property adds another layer of exposure. However, it also provides opportunities to build resilience. A well-diversified portfolio with strong cash flow, adequate reserves, and strategic financing can withstand challenges and continue to perform over time. The goal is not to eliminate risk entirely—that is impossible—but to manage it in a way that allows you to grow confidently.

Another important aspect of managing risk is maintaining flexibility. This means having multiple exit strategies for each property. For example, if short-term rental demand declines, can the property be converted into a long-term rental? If market conditions change, can you sell the property at a profit? Having these options provides a safety net and allows you to adapt to changing परिस्थितations without being forced into unfavorable decisions.

Stress testing your portfolio is a valuable exercise that many investors overlook. This involves analyzing how your properties would perform under different scenarios, such as a 20% drop in revenue, a period of extended vacancy, or an increase in interest rates. By understanding how your portfolio responds to these challenges, you can identify potential weaknesses and take steps to address them before they become problems.

Ultimately, managing risk when leveraging equity is about balance. It is about finding the right combination of growth and stability, where you can take advantage of opportunities without exposing yourself to unnecessary danger. The most successful Airbnb investors are not those who take the biggest risks, but those who take calculated risks and manage them effectively.

As you continue to scale your Airbnb portfolio, remember that leverage is a tool, not a guarantee of success. It must be used with discipline, strategy, and a clear understanding of the potential outcomes. By prioritizing risk management, you ensure that your growth is sustainable and that your portfolio can weather the inevitable ups and downs of the market.

Real Life Math Example: Managing Risk in a Leveraged Airbnb Portfolio

Consider an investor named Lisa who owns three Airbnb properties. Each property is valued at $500,000, giving her a total portfolio value of $1.5 million. She has refinanced her properties and carries an average loan balance of $375,000 on each, resulting in total debt of $1.125 million. Her combined equity is $375,000.

Each property generates an average monthly revenue of $6,000, for a total of $18,000 per month across the portfolio. After expenses, including cleaning, utilities, maintenance, and management, her net operating income is $12,000 per month.

Her total monthly mortgage payments are $9,000, leaving her with $3,000 in net cash flow.

At first glance, Lisa's portfolio appears strong. However, she wants to evaluate her risk exposure. She calculates her overall DSCR by dividing her net operating income by her debt service. $12,000 divided by $9,000 equals a DSCR of 1.33. This indicates a reasonable safety margin, but not an excessive one.

Lisa then performs a stress test by assuming a 20% drop in revenue due to seasonal fluctuations or market changes. Her monthly revenue would decrease from $18,000 to $14,400. After expenses, her net operating income would drop to approximately $9,600. With mortgage payments still at $9,000, her cash flow would shrink to $600 per month.

If revenue were to drop by 30%, her monthly income would fall to $12,600, with net operating income of around $8,400. In this scenario, her income would no longer fully cover her mortgage payments, resulting in a monthly deficit of $600. This highlights the importance of maintaining reserves and conservative leverage.

Lisa currently has $30,000 in reserves, which covers approximately three months of expenses. Based on her stress test, she decides to increase her reserves to $50,000 to provide a greater safety margin. She also explores ways to improve her properties' performance, such as enhancing amenities and optimizing pricing, to increase revenue and strengthen her DSCR. Additionally, Lisa considers diversifying her portfolio by acquiring a property in a different market with a different demand profile. This reduces her reliance on a single location and helps balance seasonal fluctuations.

Through this analysis, Lisa gains a clear understanding of her risk exposure and takes proactive steps to strengthen her portfolio. By maintaining strong cash flow, adequate reserves, and diversified investments, she positions herself to handle challenges while continuing to grow.

This example demonstrates that managing risk is not about avoiding leverage, but about using it wisely. By understanding the numbers and preparing for different scenarios, investors can build resilient portfolios that generate consistent income and long-term wealth.

Chapter 8

Building a Long-Term Refinance Strategy for Airbnb Wealth

As you reach this stage in your Airbnb investing journey, it becomes clear that refinancing is not just a tactical move—it is a long-term strategy that must be integrated into your overall wealth-building plan. Many investors approach refinancing as a one-time event, triggered by a need for cash or a favorable interest rate environment. However, the most successful Airbnb investors think of refinancing as an ongoing system, one that is carefully planned, executed, and repeated over time to optimize capital, improve cash flow, and scale their portfolios efficiently. This chapter focuses on how to build a long-term refinance strategy that supports sustainable growth and lasting wealth.

At the heart of a long-term refinance strategy is the concept of intentional planning. Each property you acquire should be evaluated not only for its immediate cash flow potential but also for its future refinance potential. This means selecting properties in markets with strong appreciation trends, high demand for short-term rentals, and the ability to increase income through optimization. From the moment you purchase a property, you should already be thinking about how and when you will refinance it, what metrics you need to achieve, and how the proceeds will be used.

A key component of this strategy is creating a refinance timeline for each property. This timeline outlines the expected progression from acquisition to stabilization, and ultimately to refinancing. For example, you may plan to acquire a property, spend three to six months optimizing it, and then hold it for an additional six to twelve months to establish consistent income. Once the property meets your performance targets, you can initiate the refinance process. By mapping out this timeline in advance, you create a structured approach that reduces uncertainty and improves execution.

Another important element is aligning your refinance strategy with your overall portfolio goals. Whether your objective is rapid expansion, steady cash flow, or a balance of both, your refinancing decisions should support that vision. For instance, if your goal is to scale quickly, you may prioritize cash-out refinances to access capital for new acquisitions. If your focus is on stability, you may emphasize rate-and-term refinances to improve cash flow and reduce risk. Understanding your priorities allows you to make more informed decisions and avoid conflicting strategies.

Portfolio sequencing is also a critical aspect of long-term refinance planning. As you acquire multiple properties, you must decide the order in which they will be refinanced and how the proceeds will be allocated. This requires a strategic approach, where you identify which properties have the highest refinance potential and prioritize them accordingly. By sequencing your refinances effectively, you can create a steady flow of capital that fuels continuous growth without overextending your resources.

Tracking performance metrics is essential for executing a successful refinance strategy. These metrics include occupancy rates, average daily rates, gross revenue, net operating income, and DSCR. By monitoring these indicators, you can determine when a property is ready for refinancing and ensure that it meets lender requirements. Consistent tracking also allows you to identify areas for improvement and optimize your properties for maximum performance.

Another important consideration is lender relationships. Building strong relationships with lenders who understand the Airbnb model can provide access to better loan products, faster approvals, and more flexible terms. Over time, these relationships can become a valuable asset, enabling you to execute your strategy more efficiently. Investors who work with multiple lenders can also benefit from increased options and competitive terms, further enhancing their refinancing capabilities. As part of your long-term strategy, it is important to maintain flexibility. Market conditions, interest rates, and regulations can change, and your strategy must be adaptable to these shifts. This may involve adjusting your refinance timeline, exploring alternative financing options, or modifying your investment approach. Flexibility allows you to respond to opportunities and challenges without compromising your overall goals.

Tax efficiency is another factor that should be integrated into your refinance strategy. While refinancing itself is not typically a taxable event, the way you use the proceeds and structure your investments can have tax implications. For example, reinvesting refinance proceeds into additional properties may provide opportunities for depreciation and other tax benefits. Working with a knowledgeable tax professional can help you optimize your strategy and maximize after-tax returns.

Long-term wealth building also requires a balance between growth and stability. While refinancing can accelerate portfolio expansion, it is important to ensure that your portfolio remains financially sound. This means maintaining strong cash flow, adequate reserves, and manageable debt levels. Over time, you may choose to shift your strategy from aggressive growth to consolidation, focusing on paying down debt and increasing equity. Another advanced aspect of long-term refinance strategy is portfolio-level optimization. Instead of evaluating each property individually, you begin to look at your portfolio as a whole. This includes analyzing overall leverage, cash flow, and risk exposure. By optimizing your portfolio at this level, you can make more strategic decisions about refinancing, acquisitions, and asset allocation. This holistic approach is what distinguishes sophisticated investors from those who operate on a deal-by-deal basis.

Exit strategy planning is also an integral part of long-term refinancing. While the goal may be to build and hold a portfolio, there will come a time when you may want to sell properties, transition to different investments, or reduce leverage. Having a clear exit strategy ensures that you can capture value at the right time and adapt to changing circumstances. This may involve selling underperforming properties, refinancing into long-term fixed-rate loans, or consolidating your portfolio.

As your portfolio grows, the compounding effects of your refinance strategy become increasingly evident. Each successful refinance provides capital for new investments, which in turn generate additional income and equity. Over time, this creates a powerful cycle of growth that can lead to significant wealth accumulation. The key is to remain disciplined, strategic, and focused on long-term objectives. Ultimately, building a long-term refinance strategy is about creating a system that works for you. It is about aligning your actions with your goals, leveraging your resources effectively, and continuously improving your approach. By doing so, you can transform your Airbnb investments into a sustainable and scalable source of wealth. This is not just about making money—it is about building a financial foundation that supports your lifestyle, your ambitions, and your future.

Real Life Math Example: Long-Term Refinance Strategy in Action

Let's consider an investor named David who begins with a clear long-term refinance strategy. He purchases his first Airbnb property for $400,000, putting down $80,000 and financing $320,000. He invests $20,000 into furnishings and improvements, bringing his total investment to $100,000. Within the first year, the property generates $6,500 per month in revenue, or $78,000 annually, with a net operating income of $50,000.

After one year of strong performance, the property is appraised at $520,000. David refinances at 75% LTV, securing a loan of $390,000. After paying off the original loan, he receives approximately $70,000 in cash after closing costs. He uses this capital, along with additional savings, to purchase a second property. David repeats this process with each new acquisition, carefully timing his refinances and reinvesting the proceeds. Over five years, he acquires five properties, each valued at an average of $500,000. His total portfolio value is $2.5 million. His total loan balances amount to $1.8 million, leaving him with $700,000 in equity.

Each property generates an average net income of $2,500 per month, resulting in total monthly income of $12,500, or $150,000 annually. David uses a portion of this income to build reserves and pay down debt, while reinvesting the rest into new opportunities.

By year ten, David has refined his strategy and expanded his portfolio to eight properties. The average property value has increased to $600,000, bringing his total portfolio value to $4.8 million. His total loan balances are $3 million, and his equity has grown to $1.8 million. His monthly cash flow now exceeds $20,000.

At this stage, David begins to shift his strategy from aggressive growth to long-term stability. He focuses on rate-and-term refinances to reduce interest rates and improve cash flow. He also pays down debt on selected properties, increasing his equity and reducing risk.

This example illustrates how a long-term refinance strategy

can transform a modest initial investment into a substantial real estate portfolio. By planning each step, tracking performance, and adapting to changing conditions, David is able to build wealth steadily and sustainably.

Chapter 9

Advanced Strategies — Combining DSCR, HELOCs, and Creative Financing for Maximum Leverage

As you reach the advanced stage of Airbnb investing, refinancing alone is no longer the only tool in your financial arsenal. The most sophisticated investors combine multiple financing strategies—such as DSCR loans, HELOCs (home equity lines of credit), and creative financing—to maximize leverage, flexibility, and speed. These strategies allow you to move beyond linear growth and enter a phase of exponential scaling, where capital is continuously accessed, deployed, and recycled across multiple opportunities. In this chapter, you will learn how to integrate these tools into a cohesive strategy that enables you to close more deals, optimize your capital structure, and build a dominant Airbnb portfolio.

The foundation of this advanced approach begins with DSCR loans. Debt Service Coverage Ratio loans are uniquely suited for Airbnb investors because they focus on the property's income rather than the borrower's personal income. This allows investors to scale without being limited by traditional debt-to-income ratios. As long as your property generates sufficient income to cover its debt obligations, you can continue to qualify for additional loans. This creates a scalable financing model that aligns perfectly with the income-generating nature of short-term rentals.

However, DSCR loans alone are not enough to maximize growth. This is where HELOCs come into play. A HELOC allows you to access equity from an existing property as a revolving line of credit. Unlike a cash-out refinance, which provides a lump sum, a HELOC gives you ongoing access to funds that you can draw from as needed. This flexibility is invaluable for Airbnb investors, as it allows you to act quickly on opportunities, cover renovation costs, or bridge financing gaps without committing to a full refinance.

The combination of DSCR loans and HELOCs creates a powerful synergy. For example, you can use a HELOC to fund the down payment and initial setup costs for a new Airbnb property, then use a DSCR loan to finance the majority of the purchase. Once the property is stabilized and generating income, you can refinance it to pay off the HELOC and replenish your line of credit. This creates a continuous cycle where your capital is always in motion, enabling you to scale rapidly without depleting your reserves. Creative financing adds another layer to this strategy. This includes techniques such as seller financing, subject-to deals, private money, and partnership structures. These methods allow you to acquire properties with little or no upfront capital, further increasing your leverage and expanding your options. For instance, a seller may agree to finance a portion of the purchase price, reducing the amount you need to borrow from a traditional lender. Alternatively, a private investor may provide funds in exchange for a share of the profits. By combining these approaches with DSCR loans and HELOCs, you can structure deals that would otherwise be impossible.

One of the key advantages of using multiple financing strategies is speed. In competitive Airbnb markets, the ability to act quickly can make the difference between securing a deal and missing out. HELOCs and private money provide immediate access to capital, allowing you to make competitive offers and close deals faster. Once the property is acquired and stabilized, you can transition to longer-term financing through DSCR loans or refinances. This approach allows you to balance speed with stability.

Another important benefit is flexibility. Each financing tool has its own strengths and limitations, and combining them allows you to tailor your approach to each deal. For example, a HELOC may be ideal for short-term funding, while a DSCR loan provides long-term stability. Creative financing can fill gaps and provide solutions when traditional financing is not available. By understanding how to use each tool effectively, you can navigate complex scenarios and maximize your opportunities.

However, with increased leverage comes increased responsibility. Managing multiple financing sources requires careful planning and coordination. Each loan or credit line has its own terms, interest rates, and repayment requirements. Failing to manage these effectively can lead to cash flow issues and increased risk. This is why it is essential to maintain a clear understanding of your overall financial position and ensure that your portfolio remains sustainable.

Cash flow management becomes even more critical when using advanced financing strategies. Each property must generate sufficient income to cover its debt obligations while contributing to overall portfolio performance. This requires accurate forecasting, efficient operations, and continuous optimization. Investors must also account for the costs associated with each financing tool, including interest, fees, and potential rate adjustments.

Another key consideration is exit strategy. Advanced financing often involves short-term or variable-rate components, such as HELOCs or private money. These must eventually be replaced or paid off, typically through refinancing or property sales.

Having a clear exit plan ensures that you can transition smoothly from short-term financing to long-term stability. This reduces risk and allows you to maintain control over your portfolio.

As your portfolio grows, the integration of these strategies becomes more sophisticated. You may find yourself managing multiple properties, each with different financing structures and timelines. At this stage, organization and systems become essential. Tracking your loans, monitoring performance, and planning your next moves require a high level of discipline and attention to detail. Successful investors develop systems that allow them to manage complexity while maintaining clarity.

Risk management remains a central theme throughout this process. While advanced financing strategies can accelerate growth, they also increase exposure to market fluctuations and operational challenges. Maintaining strong reserves, conservative leverage, and diversified investments helps mitigate these risks. The goal is to build a portfolio that is both dynamic and resilient, capable of adapting to changing conditions while continuing to grow.

Ultimately, combining DSCR loans, HELOCs, and creative financing allows you to unlock the full potential of your Airbnb investments. It enables you to move beyond traditional limitations and create a system where capital is continuously recycled and redeployed. This is the level at which true portfolio scaling occurs, where each deal builds upon the last and your growth becomes self-sustaining.

This is not just about acquiring more properties—it is about mastering the financial architecture behind your portfolio. By understanding how to structure deals, manage leverage, and optimize your capital, you position yourself as a strategic investor capable of navigating complex opportunities and achieving long-term success.

Real Life Math Example: Combining DSCR, HELOC, and Creative Financing

Let's consider an investor named Ryan who owns an Airbnb property valued at $600,000 with a loan balance of $400,000. He has $200,000 in equity. Ryan opens a HELOC on the property, allowing him to access up to 80% of the property's value. This gives him a credit line of $480,000, minus the existing loan, resulting in $80,000 of available HELOC funds.

Ryan identifies a new Airbnb property priced at $500,000. Instead of using his own cash, he draws $75,000 from his HELOC to cover the down payment and initial setup costs. He then secures a DSCR loan for the remaining $425,000. The property is acquired with minimal out-of-pocket investment.

After optimizing the property, Ryan generates $7,000 per month in revenue, with net operating income of $4,500. He stabilizes the property over 12 months and obtains a new appraisal, valuing the property at $650,000. He then performs a cash-out refinance at 75% LTV, securing a new loan of $487,500.

After paying off the original DSCR loan of $425,000, Ryan receives $62,500 in cash. He uses this amount to pay down the HELOC balance, reducing his outstanding credit line and restoring available funds. This effectively recycles his capital, allowing him to repeat the process.

Now, Ryan still owns both properties. The first property generates $6,000 per month in revenue, while the second generates $7,000. His total monthly revenue is $13,000, with strong cash flow after expenses and debt service.

Ryan then identifies a third opportunity. He partners with a private investor who contributes $50,000 in exchange for a share of the profits. Ryan combines this with funds from his HELOC to acquire another property, again using a DSCR loan for the majority of the financing.

Over time, Ryan builds a portfolio of four properties using this combined strategy. Each property generates an average net income of $2,500 per month, resulting in total monthly cash flow of $10,000. His portfolio value exceeds $2.5 million, with significant equity and multiple financing tools at his disposal.

This example demonstrates how combining DSCR loans, HELOCs, and creative financing can dramatically accelerate portfolio growth. By leveraging multiple sources of capital and recycling funds efficiently, Ryan is able to scale quickly while maintaining control over his investments.

Chapter 10

Putting It All Together — The Ultimate Airbnb Refinance & Scaling Blueprint

At this stage in your journey, you have learned the individual components of refinancing, equity extraction, risk management, timing, and advanced financing strategies. Now it is time to bring everything together into a unified system—a repeatable blueprint that allows you to consistently acquire, optimize, refinance, and scale Airbnb properties. This chapter is about integration. It is about transforming knowledge into execution and creating a structured approach that you can apply over and over again to build long-term wealth.

The ultimate Airbnb refinance and scaling blueprint begins with clarity of vision. You must define your goals: how many properties you want to own, how much monthly income you want to generate, and what level of financial freedom you are aiming for. Without a clear target, it becomes difficult to make strategic decisions. Every refinance, every acquisition, and every improvement should align with your long-term objectives. This vision becomes the foundation upon which your entire system is built. The first step in the blueprint is acquisition. You identify properties with strong short-term rental potential—locations with high demand, favorable regulations, and the ability to generate above-average income. You analyze deals based not only on purchase price but also on projected revenue, occupancy, and scalability. The goal is to acquire properties that can be optimized and refinanced, not just held passively. This requires a shift in mindset from buying properties to building assets that can be leveraged.

Once the property is acquired, the next phase is optimization. This involves transforming the property into a high-performing Airbnb through design, amenities, pricing strategies, and guest experience. The objective is to maximize revenue and create a strong performance track record. This is critical because your ability to refinance and extract equity depends heavily on the property's income and valuation. Optimization is where you create value, both in terms of cash flow and future financing potential.

After optimization comes stabilization. This is the period where the property demonstrates consistent income over time, typically six to twelve months. During this phase, you refine your operations, improve efficiency, and build a reliable income history. This stability is essential for refinancing, as lenders need to see consistent performance before approving new loans. Stabilization also provides an opportunity to identify and address any operational challenges. The next step is refinancing. Based on the property's improved value and income, you perform either a cash-out refinance to extract equity or a rate-and-term refinance to improve cash flow. The choice depends on your strategy and market conditions. Cash-out refinancing provides capital for new acquisitions, while rate-and-term refinancing enhances stability. In many cases, investors use a combination of both to balance growth and risk.

Once equity is extracted, the next phase is redeployment. This is where the blueprint becomes a cycle. The capital obtained from refinancing is used to acquire additional properties, which then go through the same process of optimization, stabilization, and refinancing. Each cycle adds to your portfolio, creating a compounding effect that accelerates growth. This is the essence of scaling—using existing assets to fuel new opportunities.

Risk management is integrated throughout every step of the blueprint. From acquisition to refinancing, you must evaluate each decision in terms of its impact on cash flow, leverage, and overall portfolio stability. Maintaining strong DSCR ratios, adequate reserves, and diversified investments ensures that your growth is sustainable. The goal is not just to expand quickly, but to build a resilient portfolio that can withstand market fluctuations.

Timing plays a crucial role in executing this blueprint effectively. Each phase must be aligned with market conditions, property performance, and your overall strategy. Refinancing too early or too late can impact your results, while acquiring properties at the wrong time can limit your potential. By staying informed and disciplined, you can optimize your timing and maximize your returns.

Another key component of the blueprint is systems and processes. As your portfolio grows, managing multiple properties and financing strategies becomes increasingly complex. Developing systems for tracking performance, managing operations, and coordinating financing allows you to maintain control and efficiency. This includes using technology, hiring support, and creating standardized processes that can be replicated across your portfolio.

The blueprint also emphasizes continuous improvement. Each cycle provides an opportunity to refine your approach, learn from experience, and improve your results. This may involve adjusting your acquisition criteria, enhancing your property design, or exploring new financing options. By continuously evolving, you stay ahead of the market and maintain a competitive advantage.

As you implement this blueprint, you begin to transition from an investor to an operator and strategist. Your focus shifts from individual deals to overall portfolio performance. You start to think in terms of systems, scalability, and long-term outcomes. This mindset is essential for building significant wealth and achieving financial independence.

Ultimately, the Airbnb refinance and scaling blueprint is about creating a self-sustaining system. Each property contributes to the acquisition of the next, each refinance unlocks new opportunities, and each improvement enhances your overall performance. Over time, this system becomes a powerful engine for wealth creation, allowing you to achieve your financial goals and create lasting impact.

Real Life Math Example: The Full Airbnb Scaling Blueprint in Action

Consider an investor named Alex who starts with a clear goal: to build a portfolio of five Airbnb properties generating $15,000 per month in net income. He begins by purchasing his first property for $400,000, putting down $80,000 and investing an additional $20,000 into setup and improvements. The property generates $6,000 per month in revenue, with net operating income of $4,000.

After one year, the property is appraised at $520,000. Alex

performs a cash-out refinance at 75% LTV, securing a loan of $390,000. After paying off the original loan, he receives $70,000 in cash. He uses this along with savings to purchase a second property.

He repeats the process, optimizing and stabilizing the second property, which generates $6,500 per month in revenue. After appreciation and income growth, the property is refinanced, providing additional capital for a third acquisition. Each cycle builds upon the previous one, creating a compounding effect.

By year four, Alex owns four properties, each generating an average net income of $2,500 per month. His total monthly income is $10,000. He continues the process, acquiring a fifth property and reaching his goal of $15,000 per month in net income.

Let's break down the numbers. Each property is valued at an average of $550,000, resulting in a total portfolio value of $2.75 million. His total loan balances are approximately $2 million, leaving him with $750,000 in equity. His monthly cash flow provides financial stability and supports further growth.

Over time, Alex begins to optimize his portfolio by refinancing into lower interest rates and improving cash flow. He also builds reserves and reduces leverage, increasing his financial security. By year ten, his portfolio has grown to seven properties, with a total value exceeding $4 million and monthly income of over $20,000. This example illustrates how the blueprint can be applied in practice. By following a structured approach and continuously reinvesting capital, Alex transforms a single property into a substantial portfolio. The key to his success is consistency, discipline, and a clear understanding of the refinancing process.

This is the power of the Airbnb refinance and scaling blueprint. It is not just a strategy—it is a system that, when executed correctly, can create long-term wealth and financial freedom.

Chapter 11

Exit Strategies — When to Sell, Refinance Again, or Hold for Long-Term Wealth

As you build and scale your Airbnb portfolio through refinancing, equity recycling, and strategic acquisitions, one of the most important questions you will eventually face is this: what is the best long-term move for each property? Should you continue holding and refinancing, sell and realize profits, or reposition the asset for a different purpose? Exit strategy is not just something you consider at the end—it is something that should be built into your investment plan from the very beginning. The most successful investors are those who understand that every property has multiple potential exit paths, and they know how to choose the right one based on timing, performance, and market conditions.

Holding a property long-term is often the most straightforward strategy, and for many investors, it is the foundation of wealth creation. By holding, you benefit from ongoing cash flow, appreciation, loan amortization, and tax advantages such as depreciation. In the Airbnb model, long-term holding can be particularly powerful because properties can generate strong income while also increasing in value over time. When combined with periodic refinancing, holding allows you to access equity without giving up ownership, creating a cycle of continuous growth.

However, holding is not always the optimal choice. Market conditions, property performance, and personal goals can all influence whether it makes sense to keep a property or sell it. For example, if a property has appreciated significantly and reached a peak value, selling may allow you to capture gains and redeploy capital into higher-performing opportunities. Similarly, if regulations change or market demand declines, selling may be a way to reduce risk and preserve capital.

Refinancing again is another powerful option that sits between holding and selling. Instead of exiting the property, you can continue to extract equity as the property appreciates and performs well. This allows you to maintain ownership while still accessing capital for new investments. Over time, this strategy can result in multiple rounds of equity extraction, each contributing to portfolio growth. The key is to ensure that each refinance strengthens your financial position and does not compromise cash flow or stability.

One of the most important factors in choosing an exit strategy is return on equity (ROE). As a property appreciates, the amount of equity you have tied up increases. However, if the property's income does not grow at the same rate, your return on that equity may decrease. In some cases, it may make sense to sell a property with high equity and reinvest the proceeds into assets with higher returns. This concept is critical for optimizing portfolio performance and ensuring that your capital is being used efficiently.

Another consideration is opportunity cost. Holding onto a property means that your capital remains tied up in that asset. If there are better opportunities available—such as higher-yielding properties or emerging markets—you must weigh the benefits of holding against the potential gains from reallocating your capital. This requires a forward-looking perspective and a willingness to adapt your strategy as conditions change.

Tax implications also play a significant role in exit decisions. Selling a property may trigger capital gains taxes, which can reduce your net proceeds. However, strategies such as 1031 exchanges can allow you to defer these taxes by reinvesting the proceeds into another property. Refinancing, on the other hand, is generally not a taxable event, making it an attractive option for accessing capital without immediate tax consequences. Understanding these implications and planning accordingly can significantly impact your overall returns.

Portfolio balance is another key factor. As your portfolio grows, you may find that certain properties no longer align with your strategy. For example, you may want to shift from smaller properties to larger, higher-end assets, or from one market to another. Selling underperforming or non-strategic properties allows you to rebalance your portfolio and focus on assets that better support your goals.

Risk management is closely tied to exit strategy as well. Holding highly leveraged properties in volatile markets can increase risk, while selling or refinancing into more stable structures can reduce exposure. Investors must continuously evaluate their risk tolerance and adjust their strategies accordingly. This includes considering factors such as interest rate changes, market cycles, and regulatory environments.

Another advanced strategy is partial liquidation, where you sell a portion of your portfolio while retaining the rest. This allows you to realize gains and reduce leverage while still maintaining income and growth potential. For example, selling one or two properties in a portfolio of five can provide significant capital for reinvestment or diversification without sacrificing overall stability.

As you gain experience, you begin to view exit strategies not as endpoints, but as transitions. Each decision—whether to hold, refinance, or sell—is part of a larger cycle of capital allocation and portfolio optimization. The goal is not just to maximize profit on individual deals, but to continuously improve the performance and structure of your entire portfolio.

Timing remains a critical element in exit strategy. Selling during a strong market can maximize returns, while refinancing during favorable interest rate conditions can improve cash flow and access capital. Monitoring market trends and staying informed allows you to act strategically rather than reactively. This proactive approach is what enables experienced investors to consistently achieve superior results.

Ultimately, the choice between holding, refinancing, or selling comes down to alignment with your long-term goals. There is no one-size-fits-all answer, and each property must be evaluated individually within the context of your overall strategy. By understanding the strengths and limitations of each option, you can make informed decisions that support your vision and maximize your wealth.

Real Life Math Example: Deciding Between Holding, Refinancing, or Selling

Consider an investor named Maria who owns an Airbnb property that she purchased for $350,000. She initially invested $70,000 as a down payment and an additional

$20,000 into improvements, bringing her total investment to $90,000. Over five years, the property has appreciated to $600,000, and her loan balance has been reduced to $280,000.

The property generates $6,500 per month in revenue, with net operating income of $4,200. Her monthly mortgage payment is $2,000, resulting in a net cash flow of $2,200 per month. Maria now has three options: hold the property, refinance it, or sell it.

If Maria chooses to hold, she continues to earn $2,200 per month, or $26,400 per year, while benefiting from ongoing appreciation and loan paydown. Her equity in the property is $320,000 ($600,000 value minus $280,000 loan). Her return on equity is approximately 8.25% ($26,400 divided by $320,000).

If Maria decides to refinance, she can access equity without selling. At 75% LTV, she qualifies for a new loan of $450,000. After paying off her existing loan, she receives $170,000 in cash before closing costs. After costs, she nets approximately $160,000. Her new loan payment increases to $3,200 per month, reducing her cash flow to $1,000 per month. However, she now has $160,000 in capital that can be used to acquire additional properties.

If Maria uses the $160,000 to purchase two additional Airbnb properties, each generating $2,000 per month in net income, her total monthly income increases to $5,000 ($1,000 from the original property plus $4,000 from the new properties). This significantly increases her overall cash flow and portfolio value.

Alternatively, Maria could choose to sell the property. After selling for $600,000 and paying off the loan, she nets approximately $300,000 after closing costs and taxes. She can then reinvest this capital into multiple new properties or other investments. If she uses the $300,000 to acquire three properties, each generating $2,500 per month, her total monthly income would be $7,500.

Each option has its advantages and trade-offs. Holding provides stability and consistent income, refinancing allows for continued ownership and capital extraction, and selling provides liquidity and the potential for higher returns through reinvestment. Maria's decision depends on her goals, risk tolerance, and market conditions.

This example illustrates the importance of evaluating exit strategies based on both financial metrics and strategic considerations. By understanding the numbers and aligning her decisions with her objectives, Maria can choose the path that best supports her long-term success.

Chapter 12

Legacy Wealth — Turning Your Airbnb Portfolio into Long-Term Financial Freedom

As you reach the final stage of this journey, your perspective begins to shift from short-term gains and rapid scaling to something much more meaningful: long-term wealth, legacy, and financial freedom. The strategies you have learned throughout this series—refinancing, equity recycling, BRRRR, cash flow optimization, and advanced financing—are not just tools for building a portfolio. They are the foundation for creating a life where your income is no longer tied to your time, where your assets work for you continuously, and where you have the ability to pass wealth, knowledge, and opportunity to future generations.

Legacy wealth is built through intentional decisions that prioritize sustainability, stability, and long-term growth. While the earlier stages of your Airbnb journey may have focused on aggressive expansion, this phase emphasizes refinement and preservation. It is about taking what you have built and transforming it into a system that can endure market cycles, economic changes, and personal transitions. This requires a deeper level of strategy, discipline, and foresight.

One of the key elements of building legacy wealth is transitioning from high leverage to balanced leverage. While leverage is essential for scaling, maintaining excessive debt over the long term can introduce unnecessary risk. As your portfolio matures, you may choose to gradually reduce leverage by paying down loans, refinancing into lower interest rates, or reallocating capital. This shift increases your equity position, improves cash flow, and enhances overall stability. The goal is to reach a point where your portfolio generates strong income with manageable or minimal debt.

Cash flow becomes the central focus in this stage. Instead of reinvesting every dollar into new acquisitions, you begin to prioritize consistent and predictable income. This income can support your lifestyle, fund other investments, or be reinvested strategically. A well-structured Airbnb portfolio can generate substantial monthly income, providing financial independence and flexibility. The emphasis is on quality over quantity—owning properties that perform reliably and contribute meaningfully to your overall financial picture.

Another important aspect of legacy wealth is diversification. While Airbnb properties may be the core of your portfolio, expanding into other asset classes can reduce risk and create additional income streams. This could include long-term rentals, commercial real estate, or even non-real estate investments such as businesses or financial assets. Diversification ensures that your wealth is not overly dependent on a single market or strategy, providing greater resilience over time.

Estate planning is a critical component of legacy building. As your portfolio grows, it becomes important to consider how your assets will be managed and transferred in the future. This may involve setting up trusts, creating wills, and establishing legal structures that protect your assets and ensure a smooth transition to your heirs. Proper planning not only preserves your wealth but also minimizes taxes and legal complications. It allows you to control how your assets are distributed and ensures that your legacy is carried forward according to your wishes.

Another powerful concept is generational wealth education. Passing down assets is important, but equally important is passing down knowledge. Teaching the next generation how to manage, grow, and protect wealth ensures that your legacy continues beyond your lifetime. This includes educating them about real estate, financial management, and the principles that guided your success. By doing so, you create a lasting impact that extends far beyond monetary value.

Portfolio optimization continues to play a role in this stage, but with a different focus. Instead of maximizing growth, you aim to maximize efficiency and stability. This may involve selling underperforming properties, consolidating assets, or refinancing into long-term fixed-rate loans. Each decision is made with the goal of strengthening your portfolio and reducing risk. The emphasis is on creating a streamlined and manageable portfolio that aligns with your long-term objectives.

Another consideration is lifestyle design. Financial freedom is not just about having money—it is about having the ability to live life on your own terms. Your Airbnb portfolio can provide the flexibility to travel, spend time with family, pursue passions, or explore new opportunities. Designing your lifestyle around your income and assets allows you to fully enjoy the benefits of your hard work and strategic planning.

Tax efficiency remains an important factor in preserving wealth. Strategies such as depreciation, cost segregation, and 1031 exchanges can help minimize tax liabilities and maximize after-tax returns. Working with experienced professionals ensures that you are taking full advantage of available opportunities and complying with regulations. This proactive approach can significantly enhance your long-term financial outcomes. Philanthropy and giving back are often integral parts of legacy wealth. As you achieve financial success, you may choose to support causes, communities, or initiatives that align with your values. This not only creates a positive impact but also adds meaning and purpose to your wealth. Giving back can take many forms, from charitable donations to mentorship and community involvement.

As your journey evolves, your role shifts from active investor to steward of wealth. You may delegate day-to-day operations, rely on professional management, and focus on strategic decisions. This transition allows you to maintain control while reducing the demands on your time. It also ensures that your portfolio continues to perform effectively without requiring constant involvement.

Ultimately, legacy wealth is about creating something that lasts. It is about building a system that generates income, preserves value, and provides opportunities for future generations. Your Airbnb portfolio becomes more than just a collection of properties—it becomes a foundation for financial independence, security, and impact.

This is the culmination of everything you have learned. From your first property to a diversified portfolio, from initial investment to long-term strategy, you have built a pathway to financial freedom. The decisions you make now will shape not only your future but also the future of those who follow. By approaching this stage with intention and clarity, you can ensure that your efforts result in lasting and meaningful wealth.

Real Life Math Example: Building Legacy Wealth with an Airbnb Portfolio

Consider an investor named Jonathan who has spent the past 10 years building an Airbnb portfolio. He owns six properties, each valued at an average of $600,000, resulting in a total portfolio value of $3.6 million. His total loan balances across all properties are $1.8 million, giving him $1.8 million in equity.

Each property generates an average monthly revenue of $7,000, with net operating income of $4,500. Across six properties, Jonathan's total monthly net operating income is $27,000. His total monthly mortgage payments are $12,000, leaving him with $15,000 in net cash flow.

At this stage, Jonathan decides to shift his focus from growth to stability. He uses a portion of his cash flow to pay down debt on two of his properties, reducing their loan balances significantly. After five years, he fully pays off one property and reduces the loan on another to $100,000. This decreases his total monthly mortgage payments to $9,000, increasing his net cash flow to $18,000 per month.

Jonathan also refinances his remaining loans into lower interest rates, further improving cash flow and reducing risk. His portfolio now generates consistent and predictable income, providing financial security and flexibility.

Let's examine his return on equity. With $1.8 million in equity and annual cash flow of $216,000 ($18,000 per month), his return on equity is 12%. This is a strong and sustainable return, especially considering the stability of his portfolio.

Jonathan decides to diversify by investing $300,000 into additional assets, such as long-term rentals and dividend-paying investments. This creates additional income streams and reduces reliance on Airbnb properties alone.

He also establishes a trust to manage his assets and ensure a smooth transition to his children. By doing so, he protects his wealth and minimizes potential legal and tax complications.

Over time, Jonathan's portfolio continues to appreciate. After another 10 years, his properties are valued at an average of $800,000, bringing his total portfolio value to $4.8 million. With reduced debt and increased equity, his financial position is stronger than ever.

Jonathan's journey demonstrates how an Airbnb portfolio can evolve from a growth-focused investment into a foundation for long-term wealth and legacy. By shifting his strategy, optimizing his portfolio, and planning for the future, he creates a system that provides both financial freedom and lasting impact.

Chapter 13

Automation, Systems, and Scaling Without Burnout

As your Airbnb portfolio grows and your refinancing strategies become more advanced, a new challenge emerges—managing complexity without becoming overwhelmed. Many investors reach a point where they are generating strong income and acquiring multiple properties, but they find themselves trapped in the day-to-day operations. What began as a path to financial freedom can quickly turn into a time-consuming business if not structured properly. This is where automation, systems, and delegation become essential. The goal is to build a portfolio that not only produces income, but does so efficiently, consistently, and with minimal direct involvement.

Automation begins with recognizing that your Airbnb portfolio is not just a collection of properties—it is a business. Like any successful business, it requires systems that can operate independently of your constant attention. This includes everything from guest communication and booking management to pricing optimization, cleaning coordination, and maintenance tracking. By implementing the right systems, you create consistency in your operations, reduce errors, and free up your time to focus on higher-level strategy.

One of the most impactful areas for automation is guest communication. Instead of manually responding to every inquiry, confirmation, and message, you can use automated messaging systems that handle the majority of interactions. These systems can send pre-written messages at key stages, such as booking confirmation, check-in instructions, and post-stay follow-ups. This not only saves time but also ensures a consistent and professional experience for every guest. Over time, this consistency leads to better reviews, higher occupancy, and increased revenue.

Dynamic pricing is another area where automation can significantly improve performance. Rather than setting static nightly rates, automated pricing tools adjust your rates based on demand, seasonality, local events, and competition. This allows you to maximize revenue during high-demand periods while remaining competitive during slower times. By leveraging data and automation, you can optimize your pricing strategy without constantly monitoring the market.

Cleaning and maintenance coordination are also critical components of a scalable system. As you acquire more properties, managing turnovers manually becomes impractical. Establishing relationships with reliable cleaning teams and using scheduling tools ensures that each property is prepared for the next guest without delays. Maintenance issues can be tracked and addressed through systems that allow for quick identification and resolution. This reduces downtime and protects your property's performance.

Standardization is a key principle in building scalable systems. Each property should follow a consistent process for setup, management, and optimization. This includes standardized furnishing packages, check-in procedures, and guest experience elements. By creating repeatable processes, you reduce decision fatigue and make it easier to manage multiple properties. Standardization also simplifies training for any team members or partners you bring on.

Delegation is the next step in scaling without burnout. While automation handles repetitive tasks, delegation allows you to offload responsibilities that require human involvement. This may include hiring property managers, virtual assistants, or local teams to handle operations. The key is to clearly define roles, responsibilities, and expectations. Effective delegation requires trust, communication, and systems that allow you to monitor performance without micromanaging.

Financial systems are equally important. As your portfolio grows, tracking income, expenses, and performance across multiple properties becomes more complex. Implementing financial management systems allows you to monitor cash flow, evaluate profitability, and make informed decisions. This includes budgeting, forecasting, and tracking key metrics such as occupancy rates and revenue per property. Having a clear financial picture ensures that your portfolio remains profitable and sustainable.

Another important aspect of scaling is time management. As an investor, your time is best spent on activities that generate the highest return, such as acquiring new properties, structuring deals, and optimizing your portfolio. By automating and delegating operational tasks, you can focus on these high-value activities. This shift in focus is what allows you to scale efficiently and achieve long-term success.

Technology plays a central role in enabling automation and systems. From property management software to pricing tools and communication platforms, the right technology can streamline your operations and enhance performance. However, it is important to choose tools that integrate well and align with your strategy. Overcomplicating your systems can create inefficiencies, so simplicity and effectiveness should be the guiding principles.

As your portfolio expands, maintaining quality becomes increasingly important. Automation and systems should enhance the guest experience, not diminish it. This means regularly reviewing your processes, gathering feedback, and making improvements. High-quality experiences lead to better reviews, repeat bookings, and increased revenue. Balancing efficiency with quality ensures that your growth is sustainable.

Scaling without burnout also requires a mindset shift. You must transition from being an operator to being a strategist. This means focusing on building systems rather than performing tasks, making decisions based on data, and continuously improving your approach. It also involves recognizing when to step back and allow your systems to operate independently. This shift is essential for maintaining balance and avoiding exhaustion.

Another important consideration is building redundancy into your systems. Relying on a single person or process can create vulnerabilities. Having backup plans, multiple vendors, and contingency strategies ensures that your operations can continue smoothly even if challenges arise. This resilience is critical for maintaining consistency and protecting your income.

Ultimately, automation, systems, and delegation are what transform your Airbnb portfolio from a job into a business. They allow you to scale efficiently, maintain high performance, and achieve the freedom that drew you to real estate investing in the first place. By building a strong operational foundation, you create a portfolio that works for you, rather than the other way around.

Real Life Math Example: Scaling with Systems and Automation

Consider an investor named Kevin who owns three Airbnb properties. Each property generates an average monthly revenue of $6,500, resulting in total monthly revenue of $19,500. After expenses, his net operating income is $12,000 per month. However, Kevin is spending approximately 30 hours per week managing guest communication, coordinating cleanings, and handling maintenance issues.

Kevin decides to implement automation and systems to improve efficiency. He invests in a property management software that automates guest messaging, booking management, and scheduling. This reduces his communication workload by 70%, saving him approximately 15 hours per week. He also hires a cleaning service for each property at a cost of $1,200 per month, ensuring consistent turnovers and reducing his involvement.

Additionally, Kevin uses a dynamic pricing tool that increases his average nightly rate by 10%. This boosts his monthly revenue from $19,500 to $21,450. After accounting for the additional costs of automation tools and cleaning services, his net operating income increases to $13,000 per month.

Now, Kevin has reduced his workload from 30 hours per week to 10 hours per week while increasing his monthly income by $1,000. This allows him to focus on acquiring new properties and expanding his portfolio.

Kevin then uses the time saved to acquire a fourth property, which generates an additional $2,500 in net monthly income. His total monthly income increases to $15,500. Because his systems are already in place, adding the new property requires minimal additional time.

Over time, Kevin continues to scale his portfolio to six properties. Each property generates an average net income of $2,500 per month, resulting in total monthly income of $15,000. His systems and team allow him to manage the entire portfolio with less than 15 hours of work per week.

Let's analyze the impact. Without systems, Kevin would need to spend approximately 60 hours per week managing six properties. With automation and delegation, he maintains a manageable workload while generating significant income. This demonstrates the power of systems in enabling scalable growth. Kevin's investment in automation and delegation not only increases his income but also improves his quality of life.

He now has the time and flexibility to focus on strategy, pursue new opportunities, and enjoy the benefits of his success.

This example highlights how building systems and leveraging automation can transform your Airbnb business. By reducing workload and increasing efficiency, you create a scalable model that supports both growth and balance.

Chapter 14

Building Your Personal Brand and Deal Flow Engine

As your Airbnb portfolio grows and your systems become more refined, one of the most powerful—and often overlooked—assets you can build is your personal brand and deal flow engine. At the highest level of investing, success is no longer just about analyzing deals or optimizing properties. It becomes about attracting opportunities, capital, partnerships, and influence. Investors who consistently find the best deals are not just searching for them—they are being brought those deals because of the brand, reputation, and systems they have built around themselves.

Your personal brand is how the market perceives you. It is your reputation, your expertise, and your visibility combined into a single force that either attracts or repels opportunities. In the Airbnb and short-term rental space, a strong personal brand positions you as an expert in financing, scaling, and operating profitable properties. This credibility opens doors to off-market deals, private funding, partnerships, and even media opportunities. Instead of chasing deals, you begin to create an environment where deals come to you. The foundation of your brand is your story and your results.

Investors, lenders, and partners are drawn to individuals who can demonstrate real experience and success. This does not mean you need to start with a massive portfolio. Even one or two successful Airbnb properties can serve as proof of concept. The key is to document your journey, share your insights, and consistently communicate the value you bring. Over time, this builds trust and authority.

Content creation is one of the most effective ways to build your brand. By sharing knowledge, strategies, and real-life examples through platforms like YouTube, Instagram, or short-form video, you position yourself as a leader in your niche. This content does not need to be complex—it simply needs to be consistent and valuable. Topics can include deal analysis, financing strategies, property tours, and lessons learned. As your audience grows, so does your influence and your ability to attract opportunities.

Your brand also extends to how you present yourself professionally. This includes your website, social media profiles, and communication style. A clean, professional online presence reinforces your credibility and makes it easier for others to connect with you. It also provides a central hub where potential partners, investors, and clients can learn more about what you do and how you can work together. As your brand grows, it naturally leads to increased deal flow. Deal flow refers to the number and quality of investment opportunities that come your way. Instead of relying solely on traditional methods such as listing platforms or brokers, you begin to receive direct opportunities from wholesalers, agents, and other investors. This access to off-market deals can significantly improve your chances of finding high-quality investments with better terms.

Building relationships is a critical component of creating a deal flow engine. This includes connecting with real estate agents, wholesalers, lenders, contractors, and other investors. Each relationship represents a potential source of opportunities. By consistently providing value, maintaining professionalism, and following through on commitments, you establish yourself as a reliable and desirable partner. Over time, these relationships become a network that continuously feeds your pipeline.

Another powerful element of your deal flow engine is direct marketing. This involves reaching out to property owners, identifying potential opportunities, and initiating conversations. Strategies can include targeted messaging, mail campaigns, or digital outreach. By combining direct marketing with your brand and network, you create multiple channels for finding deals. This diversification increases your chances of success and reduces reliance on any single source.

Partnerships also play a significant role in scaling your portfolio. Not every deal needs to be funded entirely by you. By partnering with other investors, you can access additional capital, share risk, and take on larger opportunities. Your personal brand becomes a key factor in attracting these partnerships, as others are more likely to work with someone they trust and respect. Clear communication and aligned goals are essential for successful partnerships.

Capital raising is another benefit of a strong brand. As you demonstrate your expertise and track record, you may attract individuals who are interested in investing with you. This can provide access to private capital, allowing you to scale faster and take on larger projects. However, this also comes with increased responsibility. Managing other people's money requires transparency, integrity, and a clear investment strategy.

Your deal flow engine should be supported by systems that allow you to evaluate and act on opportunities efficiently. This includes having criteria for deal selection, processes for analysis, and the ability to move quickly when a good opportunity arises. Speed and decisiveness are critical in competitive markets, and having systems in place ensures that you can act without hesitation.

Consistency is the key to building both your brand and your deal flow. This is not something that happens overnight. It requires ongoing effort, regular content creation, and continuous relationship building. However, the long-term benefits are substantial. Over time, your brand becomes an asset that generates opportunities, reduces marketing costs, and enhances your overall business.

As you continue to grow, your brand and deal flow engine become a competitive advantage. While others are searching for deals, you are attracting them. While others are struggling to find capital, you have access to it. This shift allows you to focus on higher-level strategy and long-term growth.

Ultimately, building your personal brand and deal flow engine is about creating leverage beyond your properties. It is about positioning yourself in a way that amplifies your efforts and multiplies your opportunities. This is how you move from being an investor to becoming a recognized authority and leader in your space.

Real Life Math Example: How Branding and Deal Flow Accelerate Growth

Consider an investor named Daniel who owns two Airbnb properties, each generating $2,500 per month in net income, for a total of $5,000 per month. Initially, Daniel relies on traditional methods to find deals, spending time searching listings and working with agents. On average, he finds one viable deal every six months. Daniel decides to build his personal brand by creating content around his Airbnb journey. He posts weekly videos sharing his strategies, property performance, and financing techniques. Over the course of a year, his audience grows to 10,000 followers. As a result, he begins to receive direct messages from wholesalers, agents, and property owners presenting potential deals.

Instead of finding one deal every six months, Daniel now reviews three to five opportunities per month. Out of these, he identifies one strong deal every two months. This increases his acquisition rate from two properties per year to six properties per year.

Let's analyze the impact. Each new property generates an average net income of $2,500 per month. By acquiring six properties in one year, Daniel adds $15,000 per month to his income. Combined with his existing properties, his total monthly income increases to $20,000.

Additionally, Daniel attracts a private investor who provides $200,000 in capital for future deals. This allows him to acquire larger properties and scale even faster. With access to better deals and additional capital, his portfolio grows more efficiently.

Over a three-year period, Daniel expands his portfolio to ten properties, each generating an average of $2,500 per month. His total monthly income reaches $25,000. The increased deal flow and capital access significantly accelerate his growth compared to relying solely on traditional methods.

Let's also consider equity growth. If each property is valued at $500,000, Daniel's portfolio is worth $5 million. With an average loan balance of $350,000 per property, his total debt is $3.5 million, leaving him with $1.5 million in equity.

This example demonstrates how building a personal brand and deal flow engine can dramatically increase the speed and scale of your Airbnb investments. By attracting opportunities instead of chasing them, Daniel is able to grow his portfolio more efficiently and achieve his financial goals faster.

Chapter 15

The Infinite Loop — Creating a Self-Sustaining Airbnb Wealth Machine

At the highest level of Airbnb investing, everything you have learned throughout this series converges into one powerful concept: the infinite loop. This is the stage where your portfolio no longer depends on your personal income, your savings, or even your active effort to grow. Instead, it becomes a self-sustaining system where properties generate income, income increases value, value creates equity, and equity funds new acquisitions. This continuous cycle is what transforms a collection of investments into a true wealth machine.

The infinite loop begins with understanding that every property you own has multiple roles. It is not just an income-producing asset; it is also a source of equity, a financing tool, and a stepping stone to future opportunities. When you shift your mindset to view properties in this way, you begin to unlock their full potential. Each property contributes to the growth of the next, creating a chain reaction that accelerates your portfolio expansion.

The first component of the loop is income generation. Your Airbnb properties must consistently produce strong revenue through optimized pricing, high occupancy, and excellent guest experiences. This income is the foundation of the entire system. Without it, the loop cannot function effectively. By focusing on performance and quality, you ensure that each property contributes positively to your portfolio.

The second component is value creation. As your properties generate income and improve in performance, their value increases. This can occur through market appreciation, but more importantly, through forced appreciation driven by income. In the Airbnb model, higher revenue often leads to higher valuations, particularly when lenders use income-based approaches. This creates a direct link between operational excellence and financial growth.

The third component is equity extraction. As your properties increase in value, you gain access to equity that can be extracted through refinancing or other financing tools. This equity represents stored capital that can be redeployed into new opportunities. The key is to extract this equity strategically, ensuring that your properties remain financially stable while providing the capital needed for growth.

The fourth component is reinvestment. The capital obtained from equity extraction is used to acquire additional properties, which then enter the same cycle of income generation, value creation, and equity extraction. This reinvestment is what drives the loop forward, creating a compounding effect that accelerates your portfolio growth over time.

When these four components—income, value, equity, and reinvestment—are aligned, the result is a self-sustaining system. Each cycle strengthens the next, and your portfolio begins to grow organically. This is the point where you are no longer limited by your initial capital. Instead, your assets themselves become the engine of growth.

However, building an infinite loop requires precision and discipline. Each step must be executed effectively, and each decision must support the overall system. Poor property performance, excessive leverage, or misaligned financing can disrupt the loop and create vulnerabilities. This is why maintaining strong fundamentals—cash flow, reserves, and risk management—is essential.

Another important aspect of the infinite loop is scalability. As your portfolio grows, the impact of each cycle becomes more significant. A single refinance or acquisition can have a substantial effect on your overall income and equity. This scalability allows you to achieve exponential growth, where each additional property contributes more than the last. Time is a critical factor in this process. The infinite loop is not built overnight. It requires patience, consistency, and a long-term perspective. Each cycle takes time to complete, from acquisition to stabilization to refinancing. However, as you gain experience and refine your systems, the speed and efficiency of each cycle improve, allowing you to accelerate your growth.

Leverage plays a central role in the infinite loop, but it must be managed carefully. While leverage enables growth, it also introduces risk. Maintaining a balance between growth and stability ensures that your loop remains sustainable. This includes monitoring your DSCR, maintaining reserves, and avoiding overextension.

Another key element is adaptability. Markets change, interest rates fluctuate, and regulations evolve. Your infinite loop must be flexible enough to adapt to these changes. This may involve adjusting your strategy, exploring new markets, or modifying your financing approach. By staying informed and responsive, you can maintain the strength and continuity of your system.

As your portfolio reaches a certain scale, the loop begins to generate not only growth but also significant income. This income can be used to further accelerate your investments, reduce debt, or support your lifestyle. At this stage, you have achieved a level of financial independence where your assets provide both security and opportunity. The infinite loop also creates optionality. You are no longer forced to pursue growth at all costs. You can choose to slow down, consolidate, or diversify based on your goals. This flexibility is one of the greatest advantages of building a self-sustaining system. It allows you to align your investments with your life, rather than the other way around.

Ultimately, the infinite loop represents the culmination of your Airbnb investing journey. It is the point where your knowledge, strategy, and execution come together to create a system that works for you continuously. It is not just about building wealth—it is about creating a structure that can sustain and grow that wealth over time.

This is the level where true financial freedom is achieved. Your portfolio becomes more than a source of income—it becomes a legacy, a platform for future opportunities, and a testament to the power of strategic investing. By mastering the infinite loop, you position yourself to achieve long-term success and create lasting impact.

Real Life Math Example: The Infinite Loop in Action

Consider an investor named Michael who starts with one Airbnb property purchased for $400,000. He invests $100,000 total, including down payment and setup costs. The property generates $6,000 per month in revenue, with net operating income of $4,000.

After one year, the property is valued at $520,000. Michael performs a cash-out refinance at 75% LTV, securing a loan of $390,000. After paying off the original loan, he receives $70,000 in cash. He uses this to acquire a second property.

Now, Michael owns two properties, each generating $4,000 in net income. His total monthly income is $8,000. After another year, both properties appreciate to $550,000 each. He refinances one property, extracting $80,000, and uses it to acquire a third property.

With three properties, his monthly income increases to $12,000. Each property continues to generate income and build equity. After another cycle, he refinances again, acquiring a fourth property.

By year five, Michael owns five properties, each generating $4,000 per month in net income. His total monthly income is $20,000. His portfolio value is approximately $2.75 million, with significant equity.

Let's examine the loop mathematically. Each property contributes to the next through equity extraction. If each refinance yields an average of $75,000 and each new property requires $75,000 to acquire, the system becomes self-sustaining. Michael no longer needs to inject new capital—his properties fund his growth.

Over time, as property values increase and income grows, the amount of equity available for extraction also increases. This allows Michael to acquire properties more quickly, accelerating the loop. By year ten, he owns eight properties, generating $32,000 per month in net income.

His portfolio value exceeds $5 million, with equity of over $2 million. The loop continues to operate, providing both growth and income. Michael now has the option to continue expanding, reduce leverage, or enjoy the financial freedom his portfolio provides.

This example illustrates how the infinite loop transforms a single investment into a powerful wealth-building system. By aligning income, value, equity, and reinvestment, Michael creates a cycle that sustains and accelerates itself over time.

Final Thoughts

As you reach the end of this journey, it is important to pause and reflect on what you have truly built—not just in terms of knowledge, but in terms of mindset, strategy, and opportunity. This series was never just about Airbnb properties or mortgage loans. It was about understanding how money moves, how assets grow, and how everyday individuals can create extraordinary financial outcomes by applying the right principles with consistency and discipline. You have moved from learning how to qualify for a loan to understanding how to design a system that can generate income, build equity, and scale into long-term wealth.

What began as a simple concept—buying a property and renting it out—has evolved into a sophisticated strategy involving refinancing, equity extraction, portfolio scaling, risk management, and automation. You have seen how each piece connects to the next, forming a complete ecosystem where every decision influences your future growth. This interconnected understanding is what separates casual investors from those who build lasting wealth. It is not about one deal, one property, or one moment—it is about creating a repeatable process that works over time. One of the most powerful realizations you should take from this journey is that capital is not limited to what you have saved. Capital can be created. Through appreciation, income optimization, and strategic refinancing, you can unlock resources that were previously hidden within your properties. This is the foundation of scaling. Instead of waiting years to accumulate savings, you use the performance of your assets to generate new opportunities. This shift in thinking is what allows you to accelerate your progress and break free from traditional financial limitations.

At the same time, you have learned that growth without structure can lead to instability. Every strategy in this series—whether it is the BRRRR method, cash-out refinancing, or advanced financing—comes with both opportunity and responsibility. The importance of cash flow, reserves, and risk management cannot be overstated. Sustainable growth requires balance. It requires you to make decisions not only based on potential upside, but also on long-term resilience. This is what ensures that your portfolio can withstand challenges and continue to perform over time.

You have also seen how timing plays a critical role in success. Markets change, interest rates fluctuate, and opportunities come and go. The ability to recognize the right moment to act—and the discipline to wait when necessary—is a skill that develops with experience. By staying informed, analyzing data, and trusting your strategy, you can make decisions that align with your goals and maximize your outcomes. Timing is not about perfection; it is about preparation and awareness.

Another key takeaway is the importance of systems and scalability. As your portfolio grows, your role evolves. You move from being hands-on in every detail to building systems that allow your business to operate efficiently. Automation, delegation, and standardization become essential tools for maintaining performance while freeing up your time. This is where the true freedom of real estate investing begins—not just in financial terms, but in lifestyle as well.

Your personal brand and network also emerge as powerful assets. The relationships you build, the reputation you create, and the value you provide to others all contribute to your long-term success. Opportunities begin to flow toward you, partnerships become more accessible, and your influence expands. This is a form of leverage that goes beyond money—it is the ability to attract and multiply opportunities through trust and credibility.

As you continue forward, you will face decisions about when to hold, when to refinance, and when to sell. These choices will shape your portfolio and your financial future. There is no single correct path, only the path that aligns with your goals, values, and circumstances. By understanding the trade-offs and evaluating each decision carefully, you can navigate these choices with confidence and clarity.

Over time, your focus may shift from rapid growth to long-term stability and legacy. This is a natural progression. The same strategies that helped you build your portfolio can be adapted to preserve and enhance it. Paying down debt, optimizing cash flow, and diversifying your investments allow you to create a foundation that supports not only your own future, but also the future of those around you. This is where your efforts begin to take on a deeper meaning.

The concept of the infinite loop—where income creates value, value creates equity, and equity fuels new investments—represents the culmination of everything you have learned. It is a system that, once established, can operate continuously, generating both growth and income. This is the point where your portfolio becomes self-sustaining, where your assets work for you without constant input. Achieving this level of efficiency is not easy, but it is possible with dedication and strategic execution.

It is also important to recognize that this journey is not linear. There will be challenges, setbacks, and moments of uncertainty. Deals may not go as planned, markets may shift, and unexpected events may arise. These experiences are part of the process. They provide valuable lessons and opportunities for growth. The key is to remain adaptable, learn from each experience, and continue moving forward.

Your success in Airbnb investing is not determined by a single decision, but by the accumulation of many decisions over time. Each property you acquire, each refinance you execute, and each system you implement contributes to your overall trajectory. Consistency and persistence are what turn small actions into significant results. By staying committed to your strategy and continuously improving, you can achieve outcomes that may have once seemed out of reach.

As you apply these principles, remember that financial freedom is not just about numbers. It is about creating options. It is about having the ability to choose how you spend your time, where you focus your energy, and what kind of life you want to build. Your Airbnb portfolio is a tool that can help you achieve this freedom, but it is ultimately up to you to define what that freedom looks like.

Looking ahead, the opportunities in the short-term rental market continue to evolve. New technologies, changing travel patterns, and emerging markets all present possibilities for growth. By staying curious, informed, and proactive, you can continue to adapt and thrive in this dynamic environment. The strategies you have learned provide a strong foundation, but your willingness to learn and innovate will determine your long-term success.

In the end, the true value of this journey lies not just in the properties you own or the income you generate, but in the transformation that takes place along the way. You become more knowledgeable, more strategic, and more confident in your ability to navigate complex financial decisions. You develop a mindset that sees opportunities where others see obstacles, and you build a system that allows you to turn those opportunities into reality.

This is your blueprint. It is now up to you to execute it, refine it, and make it your own. Every step you take from here builds upon what you have learned. Every decision you make shapes your future. And every action you take brings you closer to the life you envision.

The path is clear. The tools are in your hands. Now it is time to move forward and create the results that are waiting for you.

How to Get a Personalized Airbnb Mortgage Loan Review

If you found this book helpful, you may want to see how these strategies apply to your own financial situation and investment goals. Every investor's profile is unique. Property type, location, projected Airbnb income, credit score, available capital, and lending guidelines all impact what loan programs you may qualify for and how your deal can be structured.

The examples in this book are designed to teach how Airbnb mortgage loans work—but your real options can only be determined by reviewing your specific numbers and investment scenario.

You can request a no-obligation Airbnb mortgage loan consultation here:

Email: info@FinibiMortgage.com

A licensed mortgage professional will review your scenario and explain what Airbnb financing options may be available to you, including DSCR loans, Non-QM programs, and alternative qualification strategies based on your property and financial profile.

No cost. No pressure. No obligation.

Sincerely,

Joseph G. Correa

Licensed Mortgage Loan Originator

Finibi Mortgage Inc.

About the Author

Joseph G. Correa is a licensed mortgage broker and the founder of Finibi Mortgage, a Florida-based brokerage specializing in real estate investment financing, Airbnb and short-term rental loans, and alternative lending strategies for investors, entrepreneurs, and self-employed borrowers. With more than two decades of experience in mortgage lending, underwriting, and financial structuring, Joseph has helped thousands of clients secure funding using intelligent, flexible loan strategies designed for modern real estate investing.

Unlike traditional loan officers who focus only on closing transactions, Joseph's approach is rooted in long-term wealth building. He believes that mortgage financing—especially for Airbnb and investment properties—should be used as a strategic tool to generate cash flow, scale portfolios, and create financial independence. His philosophy centers on using leverage intelligently, allowing investors to grow without relying solely on personal income or traditional lending limitations.

Joseph is widely recognized for his expertise in DSCR loans, Non-QM lending, short-term rental financing, bank statement programs, and creative deal structuring. He specializes in helping investors qualify based on property income rather than personal income, making it possible for beginners, self-employed individuals, and experienced investors to acquire and scale Airbnb portfolios. His ability to simplify complex lending concepts into clear, actionable strategies has empowered countless individuals to enter the real estate market with confidence.

Joseph created *The Airbnb Mortgage Loan Mastery Series* to give investors the same financing knowledge used by banks, private lenders, and institutional real estate operators. His mission is simple: to help people understand how to qualify, structure deals, and scale using modern lending strategies—so they can build profitable Airbnb businesses and long-term wealth.

When he is not structuring deals or writing, Joseph works directly with investors and borrowers across the United States to design customized financing strategies that align with their goals, property types, and growth plans.

The Airbnb Mortgage Loan Mastery Series Roadmap

The Professional Guide to Financing, Scaling, and Profiting from Short-Term Rental Properties

The purpose of *The Airbnb Mortgage Loan Mastery Series* is to give investors the same financing strategies used by banks, lenders, and institutional real estate operators—translated into clear, practical guidance for everyday investors. Each book builds on the last, taking you from foundational knowledge to advanced deal structuring, portfolio scaling, and long-term wealth creation using Airbnb and short-term rental properties.

Book 1 — Airbnb Mortgage Loan Fundamentals
This book gives you the foundation. You will understand how Airbnb mortgage loans work, what makes them different from traditional financing, and how lenders evaluate short-term rental properties. You will learn the core concepts of DSCR, Non-QM loans, and income-based qualification, along with who qualifies and how to structure your first deal. Every book that follows builds on this knowledge and shows you how to apply it to real-world investing.

Book 2 — DSCR Airbnb Mortgage Loans
This book focuses on one of the most powerful tools in Airbnb investing: DSCR loans. You will learn how to qualify using rental income instead of personal income, how DSCR is

calculated using short-term rental data, and how to position your property to meet lender requirements. This book shows you how to break free from traditional income limitations and scale faster.

Book 3 – Airbnb Mortgage Loans for Beginners This book is designed for first-time investors. You will learn how to buy your first Airbnb property using the right loan strategy, how to analyze deals, and how to overcome common obstacles. It provides a clear, step-by-step path from zero experience to your first successful investment.

Book 4 – Airbnb Investment Property Mortgage Loans This book focuses on scaling. You will learn how to finance multiple Airbnb properties, build a portfolio, and optimize cash flow. It introduces strategies for acquiring properties efficiently and managing them as part of a larger system.

Book 5 – Airbnb Mortgage Loans with No Income Verification

This book explores advanced qualification strategies. You will learn how to get approved without tax returns using DSCR, bank statement, and alternative documentation programs. It is designed for self-employed borrowers and investors who want flexibility in how they qualify.

Book 6 — Luxury Airbnb Mortgage Loans

This book focuses on high-end properties. You will learn how to finance luxury Airbnb investments, analyze high average daily rates, and balance risk with return. It introduces jumbo loan strategies and premium market positioning.

Book 7 — Airbnb Mortgage Loans for Vacation Homes

This book explains how to finance second homes and convert them into profitable short-term rentals. You will learn the difference between second home and investment property guidelines, along with hybrid usage strategies and compliance considerations.

Book 8 — Airbnb Mortgage Loan Refinancing & Cash-Out Strategies

This book teaches you how to unlock equity and scale faster. You will learn how to refinance Airbnb properties, execute cash-out strategies, and recycle capital into new investments.

Book 9 — Airbnb Mortgage Loans for Multi-Unit Properties

This book focuses on duplexes, triplexes, and small multifamily properties. You will learn how to finance multiple income streams within one property, analyze mixed rental models, and navigate zoning and compliance.

Book 10 — Advanced Airbnb Mortgage Loan Structuring

This book brings everything together. You will learn how to combine DSCR, asset-based, and creative financing strategies to close complex deals. It is designed for investors who want to operate at a high level and scale without limits.

This series is designed to be followed step by step or used as a reference based on your current stage. Whether you are just starting or already building a portfolio, each book provides the tools, strategies, and insights needed to move forward with clarity and confidence.

The goal is simple: to help you understand how to finance, structure, and scale Airbnb investments so you can build a profitable, long-term real estate business.

Educational & Financial Disclaimer

This book is provided for educational and informational purposes only. The author and publisher are not engaged in rendering legal, tax, accounting, investment, or financial advice. Although Joseph G. Correa is a licensed mortgage loan originator, the information in this book is intended to provide general education about Airbnb mortgage loans, DSCR financing, and short-term rental investment strategies—not personalized financial, legal, or lending advice.

Mortgage programs, underwriting guidelines, interest rates, credit requirements, and short-term rental financing options vary by lender, investor, state, and economic conditions, and may change at any time without notice. The examples, calculations, and scenarios presented in this book are hypothetical and are for illustration purposes only. They do not represent guaranteed results, loan approvals, or actual investment outcomes.

Short-term rental performance, including Airbnb income, occupancy rates, and average daily rates, is influenced by market demand, competition, seasonality, management quality, and local regulations. These factors can vary significantly and are not guaranteed. Before making any financial decisions—including purchasing an Airbnb property, applying for a DSCR or Non-QM loan, refinancing, or using real estate financing for investment purposes—readers should consult with a qualified mortgage professional, financial advisor, tax advisor, or attorney who can evaluate their specific situation.

Risk Disclosure

Real estate investing and short-term rental financing involve risk. Airbnb properties rely on variable income, which can fluctuate due to changes in demand, competition, economic conditions, and local regulations. There is no guarantee that a property will achieve projected income levels or maintain consistent occupancy.

Borrowing to purchase or refinance investment properties increases financial leverage and risk. Failure to make required mortgage payments could result in foreclosure or loss of property. DSCR and Non-QM loans may carry higher interest rates, stricter terms, or prepayment penalties, which can impact long-term profitability.

Additionally, changes in laws or regulations governing short-term rentals may affect your ability to operate a property as an Airbnb. Investors are responsible for ensuring compliance with all local, state, and federal regulations.

This book teaches structured, strategic, and responsible approaches to Airbnb financing and investing, but no strategy is risk-free. Readers are solely responsible for their financial decisions and outcomes. Neither the author nor the publisher makes any warranties, express or implied, regarding the accuracy, completeness, or applicability of the information in this book to any individual situation.

www.ingramcontent.com/pod-product-compliance
Lightning Source LLC
LaVergne TN
LVHW022224200926
848481LV00006B/2112